40 Fabulous Quick-Cut Quilts

EVELYN SLOPPY

Martingale®
& COMPANY

40 Fabulous Quick-Cut Quilts
© 2005 by Evelyn Sloppy

Martingale®
& C O M P A N Y

That Patchwork Place®

That Patchwork Place® is an imprint of
Martingale & Company®.

Martingale & Company
20205 144th Avenue NE
Woodinville, WA 98072-8478 USA
www.martingale-pub.com

Printed in China
10 09 08 07 06 05   8 7 6 5 4 3 2 1

Library of Congress Cataloging-in-Publication Data

Sloppy, Evelyn.
    40 fabulous quick-cut quilts / Evelyn Sloppy.
        p. cm.
    ISBN 1-56477-547-X
    1. Patchwork—Patterns. 2. Strip quilting—Patterns.
I. Title: Forty fabulous quick-cut quilts. II. Title.
    TT835.S627 2005
    746.46'041—dc22
                                        2004027886

CREDITS

President . . . . *Nancy J. Martin*
CEO . . . . *Daniel J. Martin*
VP and General Manager . . . *Tom Wierzbicki*
Publisher . . . . *Jane Hamada*
Editorial Director . . . . *Mary V. Green*
Managing Editor . . . . *Tina Cook*
Technical Editor . . . . *Ellen Pahl*
Copy Editor . . . . *Ellen Balstad*
Design Director . . . . *Stan Green*
Illustrator . . . . *Laurel Strand*
Text Designer . . . . *Trina Craig*
Cover Designer . . . . *Stan Green*
Photographer . . . . *Brent Kane*

MISSION STATEMENT

Dedicated to providing quality products and
service to inspire creativity.

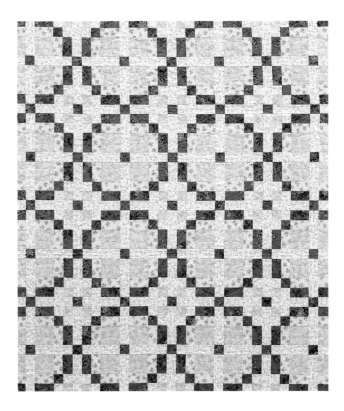

Dedication

To my girls—my daughters, Audra and Teri, my stepdaughter, Carmen, and my granddaughters, Kylie, Ireland, and Chloe.

Audra, my oldest, loves to help me in any way she can, whether it's doing my "reverse sewing," tearing off triangle papers, or ironing fabrics. She cheerfully gives up baking cookies with me when a deadline is looming. In spite of being handicapped, she recently completed her first quilt, with just a little help.

Teri, as a teenager, never thought she'd be interested in quilting. Now, as the mother of three young children, she yearns for more time to spend quilting. She very efficiently handles everything for my pattern company, Little Miss Sloppy, and her interest and knowledge in quilting is growing every day. Her first quilt was an ambitious project, a king-size quilt of many pieces with appliquéd borders, and she has gone on to make several smaller ones. Teri made "Peppermint Twist" for this book.

Carmen has just recently been bitten by the quilting bug, but she has quickly made up for lost time. Her family has retreated to the family room so that she could take over the living room for her sewing area. The room is overflowing with her fabric stash and quilting supplies. She has made many quilts and gives most of them away to friends and family. Carmen made "American Beauty" for this book.

Kylie, 15, has already made several small quilts and loves to shop for fabric with her mom. Although she has many other interests now, quilting will undoubtedly be in her future.

Ireland, 7, loves to draw pictures of quilts for me, and her designs are very original. She's a fan of the quilting show "Simply Quilts," intently watching it from beginning to end. I predict she'll be a very famous quilt designer some day.

Chloe, 2, loves to play with my scraps and all the quilts around her. I'm sure she's destined to be a quilter too.

I love to think that I started all this interest in quilting and I can relax, knowing that my quilts, quilts in progress, and fabric stash will never be sold for pennies at a garage sale.

Acknowledgments

My sincere thanks go to the following people and companies:

+ All my friends who helped by making quilts: Kathy Averett, Sherrie Boehm, Robin Bray, Carmen Christian, Marilyn Fischer, Mary Green, Teri Mayfield, Sharon Pennel, Lynda Parker, Karen Soltys, and Marge Springer.

+ All the members of my two quilting groups, Heartstring Quilters and Cowlitz Prairie Crazy Quilters. They inspire me, listen to my ideas, critique my quilts, cheer me on, and are just great friends.

+ Aptex for furnishing both batting and fabrics from Benartex, Marcus Brothers, Michael Miller, and Chanteclaire. Also thanks to AvLyn, In The Beginning Fabrics, KP Kids by Quilting Treasures, and P&B Textiles.

+ Mary Green, Karen Soltys, Terry Martin, Ellen Pahl, and the entire staff of Martingale & Company, for all the hard work they've put into making *40 Fabulous Quick-Cut Quilts*.

+ And, finally, my husband, Dean. He's a gem about keeping my quilting machine in good working order, and he even helped me out by learning to do the hand sewing on the bindings.

Contents

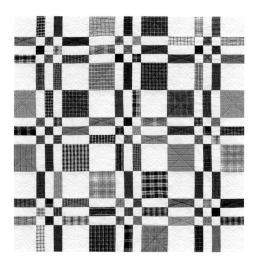

Introduction

I CAN'T THINK OF a nicer way to spend a day than attending a quilt show with my friends. We'll meet early in the morning, cups of coffee in hand, all squeeze into one car, and head for the show. Our anticipations are high, thinking about all the inspiring quilts we'll see. And we don't forget the vendors, with all the new fabrics, patterns, and supplies to entice us. I love walking down aisle after aisle of quilts. I can just feel the love that goes into making each and every one. Some quilts always stand out, the ones I know took hundreds of hours to stitch and quilt. They are real works of art, quilts to be treasured for years to come. But I find that the quilts that really tug at my heartstrings are the simpler, more traditional patterns, made from lots of warm and inviting fabrics. They just seem so cozy and comforting. They take me away from the stress of my hectic life and remind me of simpler times. These are the ones that really inspire me to go home and start yet another quilt.

Many hours later, as we all pile into our car and head for home, exhausted, visions of new quilts fill my head. How will I ever be able to make them all?

So, when I was asked if I would write a book with 40 quilts, I didn't even hesitate before giving my answer. I could make lots and lots of quilts and would not have to choose just a few to include in the book. These would be my kind of quilts, simple patterns using lots of luscious fabrics that look and feel warm and comforting. *40 Fabulous Quick-Cut Quilts* is the result—a collection of many of my favorite quilt designs. Many are my trademark scrappy quilts, while others have a more limited palette of three, four, or five fabrics. You'll find the time-saving techniques I love to use and lots of traditional patterns but with a new twist.

I hope you have as much fun making these quilts as I have. And, hopefully, I'll see some of your quilts at the next quilt show I attend, providing me with even more inspiration.

Quiltmaking Basics

Before getting started, read through this section to get a general overview of quiltmaking, especially if you are a beginner. I include helpful information on rotary cutting and accurate piecing.

ROTARY CUTTING

Instructions for quick and easy rotary cutting are provided wherever possible. All measurements include standard ¼"-wide seam allowances. For those unfamiliar with rotary cutting, a brief introduction is provided below. For more detailed information, see *Shortcuts: A Concise Guide to Rotary Cutting* by Donna Lynn Thomas (Martingale & Company, 1999).

1. Fold the fabric and match the selvages, aligning the crosswise and lengthwise grains as much as possible. On the cutting mat, place the folded edge of the fabric closest to you. Align a square ruler, such as a Bias Square®, along the folded edge of the fabric. Place a long, straight ruler to the left of the square ruler, just covering the uneven raw edges along the left side of the fabric.

2. Remove the square ruler and cut along the right edge of the long ruler, rolling the rotary cutter away from you. Discard this strip. (Reverse this entire procedure if you are left-handed.)

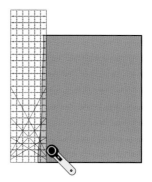

3. To cut strips, align the newly cut edge of the fabric with the appropriate ruler markings. For example, to cut a 3"-wide strip, place the 3" ruler marking at the edge of the fabric.

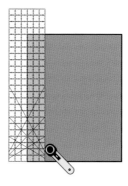

4. To cut squares, cut a strip of the required width. Trim the selvage ends and align the left edge of the strip with the desired ruler markings—the length measurement should equal the width measurement of the strip. Cut the strip into squares.

5. For rectangles, cut a strip whose width is the same as the shorter side of the desired rectangle. Use the measurement of the longer side of the rectangle when cutting the strip into rectangles. For example, to cut a 3" x 5" rectangle, cut a 3"-wide strip and then cut 5"-long segments from it.

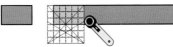

MACHINE PIECING

The most important aspect of machine piecing is maintaining a consistent ¼"-wide seam allowance. Otherwise, the quilt blocks will not be the desired finished size. If your quilt blocks finish to the wrong size, the size of everything else in the quilt will be affected, including alternate blocks, sashings, and borders. Measurements for all components of a quilt are based on blocks that finish accurately to the desired size plus ¼" on each edge for seam allowances.

Sewing Accurate Seam Allowances
Take the time to establish an exact ¼"-wide seam guide on your machine. Some machines have a special quilting foot that measures exactly ¼" from the center needle position to the edge of the foot. This feature allows you to use the edge of the presser foot to guide the fabric for a perfect ¼"-wide seam allowance. If your machine doesn't have such a foot, create a seam guide by placing the edge of a piece of tape, moleskin, or a magnetic seam guide ¼" from the needle.

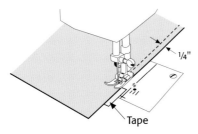

Tape

TESTING FOR ACCURACY

Do the following test to make sure you are sewing an accurate ¼"-wide seam.

1. Cut three strips of fabric, each 1½" x 3".

2. Sew the long edges of the strips together, using the edge of the presser foot or the seam guide you have made.

3. Press the seams toward the outer edges.

4. Measure the center strip. After sewing and pressing, it should measure exactly 1" wide. If it doesn't, adjust the needle or seam guide in the proper direction and repeat the test. I find that I need to sew with a scant ¼" seam (that is, about two threads less than ¼") in order for my measurements to come out correctly. This is because the pressing takes up a few threads. Try this if your sample strip is too small.

Chain Piecing
Chain piecing is an efficient system that saves time and thread. The following steps describe the process.

1. Sew the first pair of pieces from cut edge to cut edge, using 12 stitches per inch. At the end of the seam, stop sewing but do not cut the thread.

2. Feed the next pair of pieces under the presser foot, as close as possible to the first pair. Continue feeding pieces through the machine without cutting the threads in between. There is no need to backstitch, since each seam will be crossed and held by another seam.

3. When all the pieces have been sewn, remove the chain from the machine and clip the threads between the pieces.

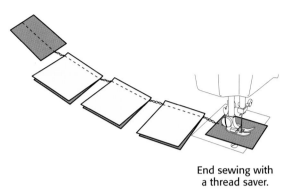

End sewing with a thread saver.

Easing

If two pieces being sewn together are slightly different in size (less than 1/8"), pin the places where the two pieces should match, and in between if necessary, to distribute the excess fabric evenly. With the longer piece on the bottom, sew the pieces together. The feed dogs will ease the extra fabric into the seam.

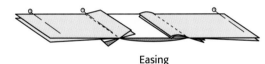

Easing

THREAD SAVERS

To save thread and prevent stray thread tails from shadowing through your quilt, use thread savers. Fold a 2" square of fabric in half (this is your first thread saver) and stitch across it from edge to edge; then with the presser foot down, feed pairs of quilt pieces through the machine as for chain piecing. When all the pieces are sewn together, sew across a second thread saver. Clip the threads between the pieces and reuse or discard the thread savers. This method eliminates trimming or having long threads hanging from your pieced blocks.

PRESSING

The traditional rule in quiltmaking is to press seams to one side, toward the darker color wherever possible. First press the seams flat from the back of the fabric; then press the seams in the desired direction from the front. Pressing is an up-and-down motion as opposed to ironing, which is a back-and-forth motion used for removing wrinkles from clothes. To avoid distorting quilt pieces, be sure to press carefully by lifting and then lowering your iron onto the pieces without moving the iron from side to side. Press the seams in the direction of the arrows in the project illustrations unless otherwise noted.

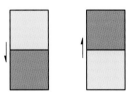

When joining two pieced units, plan ahead and press the seam allowances in opposite directions as shown. Pressing seams in opposite directions reduces bulk and makes it easier to match seam lines. Where two seams meet, the seam allowances will butt against each other, making it easier to match seam intersections perfectly.

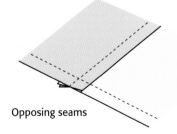

Opposing seams

Easy Piecing Techniques

To MAKE THE most of my time in the sewing room—and yours—I use streamlined piecing techniques whenever possible. I often make strip sets—long strips of fabric sewn together along their long edges—and then cut segments from them to make blocks quickly and easily. In this section, I've included the details of many other piecing tricks that are used to make the quilts in this book.

BIAS SQUARES

Bias squares are units made of two contrasting half-square triangles sewn together on their long bias edges. They are usually made by cutting half-square triangles from squares that are $7/8"$ larger than the desired finished size of the unit.

Bias Square

Stitching two triangles together on the bias can be tricky and create distorted units. I prefer to start with slightly oversized squares. I cut the squares 1" larger than the desired finished size of the unit, and then I trim them to size after I finish sewing. To make bias squares, follow the steps below.

1. Cut one square from each of two different fabrics. Cut the squares 1" larger than the desired finished size of the bias square. For example, if you want a 3" finished bias square, start with two squares, 4" x 4".

2. Place the squares right sides together and draw a diagonal line on the wrong side of one square, usually the lighter one. Stitch 1/4" away from the line on each side.

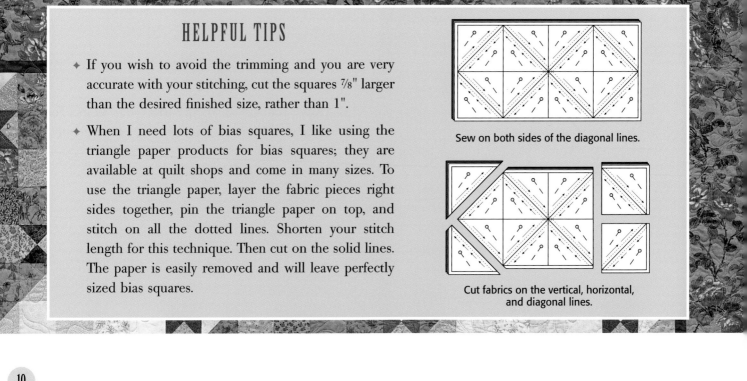

HELPFUL TIPS

+ If you wish to avoid the trimming and you are very accurate with your stitching, cut the squares $7/8"$ larger than the desired finished size, rather than 1".

+ When I need lots of bias squares, I like using the triangle paper products for bias squares; they are available at quilt shops and come in many sizes. To use the triangle paper, layer the fabric pieces right sides together, pin the triangle paper on top, and stitch on all the dotted lines. Shorten your stitch length for this technique. Then cut on the solid lines. The paper is easily removed and will leave perfectly sized bias squares.

Sew on both sides of the diagonal lines.

Cut fabrics on the vertical, horizontal, and diagonal lines.

3. Cut on the drawn line and press the seam allowances toward the darker fabric. You will have two bias squares.

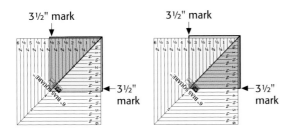

4. Using a square ruler, trim the bias squares to the correct unfinished size. Place the diagonal line of the ruler on the seam of the bias square and trim two sides as shown. Rotate the block and trim the other two sides.

QUARTER-SQUARE-TRIANGLE UNITS

The quarter-square-triangle unit is traditionally pieced by sewing four triangles together. They are usually made by cutting quarter-square triangles from squares that are cut 1¼" larger than the desired finished size of the unit.

Quarter-Square-
Triangle Unit

As with bias squares, sewing on the bias can lead to a unit that is slightly distorted or inaccurate in size. Again, I like to construct an oversized unit and then trim it down to the exact size. The beginning of the construction process is the same as for bias squares.

1. Cut two squares that are 1½" larger than the desired finished unit. For example, to make a 3" finished quarter-square-triangle unit, start with 4½" squares.

2. Follow steps 2 and 3 of "Bias Squares" on pages 10–11. Do not trim your units to size yet.

3. On the wrong side of half of the bias squares, draw a diagonal line from corner to corner as shown.

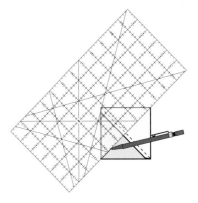

4. Pair one marked bias square with one unmarked bias square, right sides together. Make sure contrasting fabrics are facing each other and that the marked bias square is on top. Butt the diagonal seams against each other and pin to secure. Stitch ¼" away from both sides of the marked diagonal line; then cut on the drawn line. Press the seams toward one side.

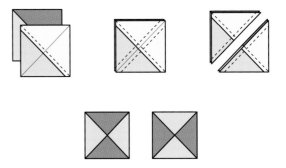

5. Now you are ready to trim your units. For example, if you would like a 3" finished unit (3½" unfinished), place the diagonal line of the square ruler on one of the seam lines. Move the ruler along the seam line until the 3½" mark on both sides of the ruler lines up where the two fabrics intersect. Trim along both edges of the ruler. Rotate your unit and trim the other two sides so that your unfinished piece is 3½". This

may take a little more effort, but your quarter-square-triangle units will be perfectly sized.

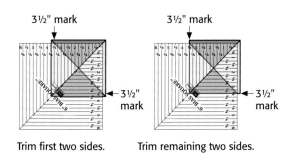

Trim first two sides.   Trim remaining two sides.

Note: *If you are very accurate with your stitching and wish to avoid trimming, cut the squares 1¼" larger than the desired finished size of the quarter-square-triangle unit, rather than 1½".*

FOLDED CORNERS

I use this technique for any fabric piece that has triangles stitched to the corners. It is more accurate to make blocks with this method because you never have to cut triangles or sew along unstable bias edges. You will start with a base piece, either a rectangle or a square, and smaller squares that will form the triangles. Sizes to cut are given in the project directions.

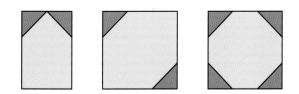

1. Draw a diagonal line from corner to corner on the wrong side of the smaller squares. Place one square on a corner of the base piece and stitch on the drawn line. Cut ¼" away from the stitching line. Press toward the triangle.

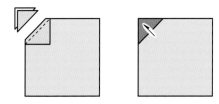

2. Follow step 1 with each corner. Some pieces may have triangles on all four corners; other pieces

may have triangles on just one, two, or three corners.

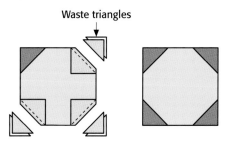

Waste triangles

FLYING GEESE BLOCKS

This is an easy, fast, and accurate way to make Flying Geese blocks. You will make four blocks at once. For greatest accuracy, I like to make the blocks oversized and then trim them to the exact size I need.

Flying Geese

1. You will start with a large square, which will be the "geese," and four smaller squares, which will be the "sky" triangles. The large square should be 1½" larger than the longest measurement of the finished Flying Geese blocks. The smaller squares should be 1" larger than the shortest measurement of the finished Flying Geese blocks. For example, 2" x 4" Flying Geese blocks (finished size) will need one large square, 5½" x 5½", and four smaller squares, 3" x 3".

2. Draw a diagonal line on the wrong side of all of the smaller squares. Place two smaller squares on top of the large square, right sides together, so that the smaller squares are on opposite diagonal corners. Stitch ¼" away from both sides of the marked diagonal lines and then cut on the drawn lines. Press the seam allowances toward the small triangles.

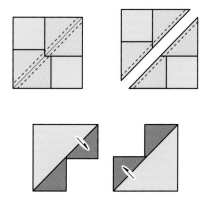

READY-MADE BIAS SQUARES

If the waste triangles from the folded corner technique are small, I discard them. If they are larger, you can use them for making bias squares. I often use them within the same quilt or save them for another project. You can make a bias square at the same time as a folded corner and thus avoid sewing triangles later on. To do this, draw a second line ½" away from the first diagonal line. Stitch on both drawn lines. Align the ¼" line of a rotary-cutting ruler along the inner seam and trim. The waste section is now a ready-made bias square.

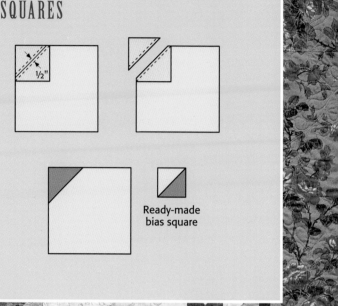

Ready-made bias square

3. Place another smaller square on the remaining corner of the large triangle. Stitch ¼" away from both sides of the marked diagonal line and then cut on the drawn line. Repeat with the remaining smaller square and large triangle. Press the seam allowance toward the small triangle. You will have four Flying Geese blocks.

4. Trim the Flying Geese blocks to the proper unfinished size, being sure to keep a ¼" seam allowance beyond the peak. The seams should end at the bottom corners.

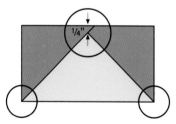

Note: *If you wish to avoid the trimming and are very accurate with your stitching, cut the large square 1¼" larger than the longest measurement of the finished Flying Geese block, and the smaller squares ⅞" larger than the shortest measurement of the finished Flying Geese block.*

Assembly and Finishing

AFTER YOU'VE PIECED all the blocks for your quilt, it's time to arrange them for the quilt you are making. If your blocks are scrappy, it's very helpful to use a design wall to arrange them into rows before sewing them together. In addition to the blocks, some quilts include sashing between the blocks and any number of inner and outer borders around the blocks. For best results, give your blocks a careful pressing and square them up before sewing them into rows.

SQUARING UP BLOCKS

When your blocks are complete, take the time to square them up. Use a large square ruler to measure your blocks and make sure they are the desired size plus an exact ¼" on each edge for seam allowances. For example, if you are making blocks that finish at 8½" square, they should all measure 9" x 9" before you sew them together. Trim larger blocks to match the size of the smallest one. Be sure to trim all four sides; otherwise your block will be lopsided.

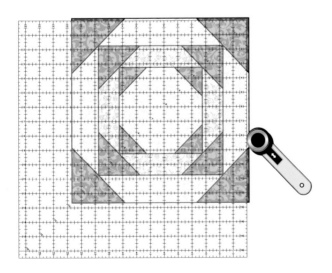

Note: *If your blocks are not the required finished size, adjust all the other components of the quilt accordingly.*

MAKING STRAIGHT-SET QUILTS

1. Arrange the blocks as indicated in the directions for each quilt project.

2. Sew the blocks together in horizontal rows; press the seams in opposite directions from row to row.

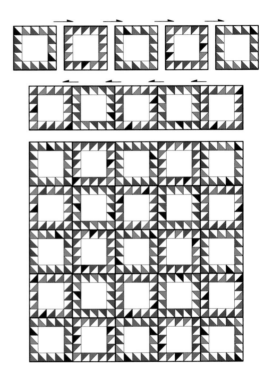

3. Sew the rows together, making sure to match the seams between the blocks.

MAKING DIAGONALLY SET QUILTS

1. Arrange the blocks and setting triangles as indicated for each quilt project.

2. Sew the blocks together in diagonal rows; press the seams in opposite directions from row to row.

3. Sew the rows together, making sure to match the seams between the blocks. Sew the corner setting triangles last.

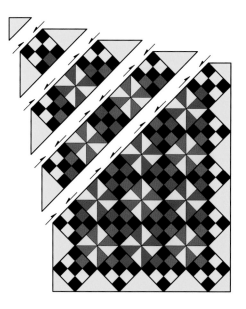

ADDING BORDERS

For best results, do not cut border strips and sew them directly to the quilt sides without measuring first. Since the edges of a quilt often measure slightly longer than the distance through the quilt center due to stretching during construction, measure the quilt top through the center in both directions instead of the edges to determine how long to cut the border strips. This step ensures that the finished quilt will be as straight and as square as possible, without wavy edges.

Plain border strips are commonly cut along the crosswise grain of fabric and seamed as needed for lengths longer than 40". Borders cut from the lengthwise grain of fabric require extra yardage, but seaming the required length is then unnecessary. Borders cut from the lengthwise grain also have less stretch than borders cut from the crosswise grain and will be less likely to have wavy edges. You may add borders that have straight-cut corners or mitered corners.

Straight-Cut Borders

1. Measure the length of the quilt top through the center. Cut two border strips to this measurement, piecing as necessary. Mark the center of the quilt edges and the border strips. Pin the borders to the sides of the quilt top, matching the center marks and ends and easing as necessary. Sew the border strips in place using a ¼" seam allowance. Press the seams toward the border strips.

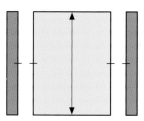

Mark centers.

TRIMMING TRIANGLES

I USUALLY CUT setting triangles larger than necessary and trim them after the quilt top is assembled. The cutting dimensions given for all the setting triangles in this book are slightly oversized. To trim the edges of the quilt, use a long cutting ruler and rotary cutter. In general, align the ¼" mark on the ruler with the block points and trim the quilt edges.

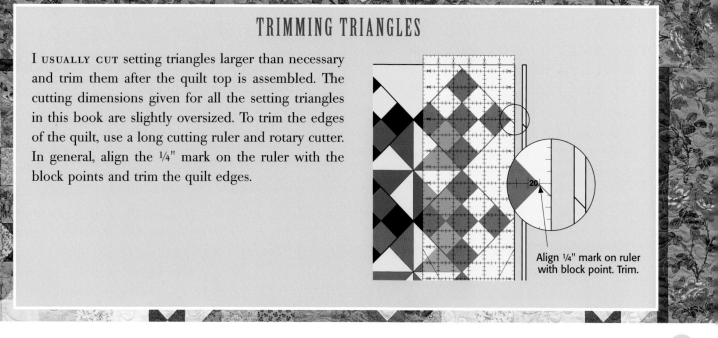

Align ¼" mark on ruler with block point. Trim.

2. Measure the width of the quilt top through the center, including the side borders just added. Cut two border strips to this measurement, piecing as necessary; mark the center of the quilt edges and the border strips. Pin the borders to the top and bottom edges of the quilt top, matching the center marks and ends and easing as necessary; stitch. Press the seams toward the border strips.

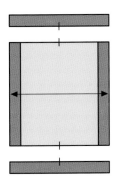

Measure center of quilt,
side to side, including borders.
Mark centers.

Mitered Borders

1. First estimate the finished outside dimensions of your quilt, including the borders. For example, if your quilt top measures 35½" x 50½" across the center and you want a 5"-wide finished border, your quilt will measure 45½" x 60½" after the borders are attached. Add ½" to the width and 3" to 4" to the length measurements, and cut the border strips to these estimated dimensions. The extra length will give you some leeway when folding and stitching the miters.

2. Fold the quilt in half and mark the center of the quilt edges. Fold each border strip in half and mark the center with a pin.

3. Measure the length and width of the quilt top across the center. Note the measurements.

4. Place a pin at each end of the side border strips to mark the length of the quilt top. Repeat with the top and bottom borders.

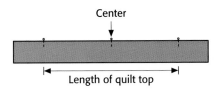

Center

Length of quilt top

5. Pin the borders to the quilt top, matching the centers. Line up the pins at each end of the border strip with the edges of the quilt. Stitch, beginning and ending the stitching ¼" from the raw edges of the quilt top. Repeat with the remaining borders.

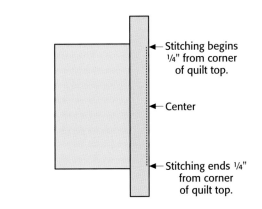

Stitching begins ¼" from corner of quilt top.

Center

Stitching ends ¼" from corner of quilt top.

6. Lay the first corner to be mitered on the ironing board. Fold under one border strip at a 45° angle to the other strip. Press and pin.

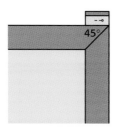

7. Fold the quilt with right sides together, lining up the edges of the border. If necessary, use a ruler to draw a pencil line on the crease to make the line more visible. Stitch on the crease, sewing from the corner to the outside edge.

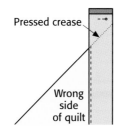

Pressed crease

Wrong side of quilt

8. Press the seam open and trim away the excess border strips, leaving a ¼"-wide seam allowance.

9. Repeat with the remaining corners.

LAYERING AND BASTING

Choose your batting and piece the backing fabric as needed. I've allowed enough yardage for the backing fabric in the project materials lists so that you can have a 4" margin around all sides of the quilt top if desired. The batting sizes allow for 2" on all sides.

If you plan to mark quilting designs on your quilt, it's easier to do that before you layer it with batting and backing. Give the quilt top a final pressing and then mark the quilting designs. Test the marker you plan to use on scrap fabric first so that you know that the marks can be easily removed after quilting.

To layer your quilt, place the backing on a table with the wrong side of the fabric facing up. If the table is large enough, you may want to tape the backing down with masking tape. Spread your batting over the backing, centering it, and smooth out any folds or wrinkles. Center the pressed and marked quilt top on these two layers, right side up. Check all four sides to make sure there is adequate batting and backing. Gently stretch the backing to make sure it is still smooth.

Once your quilt is layered, you can baste the quilt. The basting method you use depends on whether you will quilt by hand or by machine. Thread basting is generally used for hand quilting, while safety-pin basting is used for machine quilting. Space the stitching lines or pins about 4" apart.

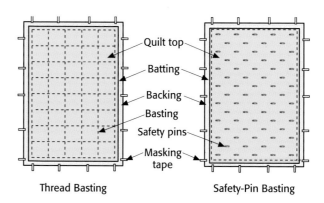

Quilt top
Batting
Backing
Basting
Safety pins
Masking tape

Thread Basting   Safety-Pin Basting

BINDING

You can use strips cut from the straight grain or bias grain of fabric to make a French double-fold binding that rolls over edges nicely and has two layers of fabric to resist wear. You will need enough strips to go around the perimeter of the quilt, plus 10" for seams and the corners in a mitered fold.

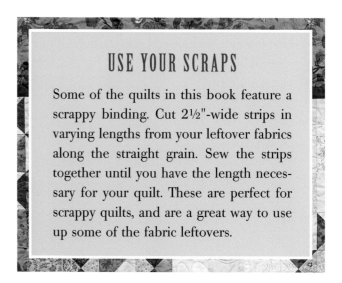

USE YOUR SCRAPS

Some of the quilts in this book feature a scrappy binding. Cut 2½"-wide strips in varying lengths from your leftover fabrics along the straight grain. Sew the strips together until you have the length necessary for your quilt. These are perfect for scrappy quilts, and are a great way to use up some of the fabric leftovers.

To make bias strips for binding, open up your binding fabric and lay it flat. Align the 45° line on your rotary-cutting ruler with one of the selvage edges of the fabric. Cut along the ruler edge and trim off the corner. Cut 2½"-wide strips, measuring from the edge of the initial bias cut. Note that for quilts with rounded corners, you will need to use binding made with bias strips.

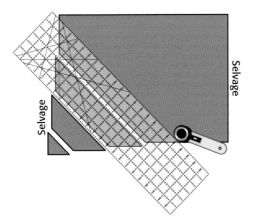

Once you cut the strips for binding, follow these steps to join the strips and attach the binding:

1. With right sides together, join the strips at right angles and stitch on the diagonal as shown. Trim the excess fabric and press the seams open to make one long piece of binding.

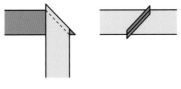

Joining Straight-Cut Strips

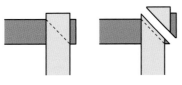

Joining Bias Strips

2. Fold the strip in half lengthwise, wrong sides together, and press.

3. Trim the batting and backing so that it extends ¼" beyond the quilt top. This extra material will fill up the binding when you attach it so that the binding isn't flat.

4. Use a walking foot, if you have one, for attaching the binding. It is helpful in feeding all the layers of the quilt evenly through the machine. Starting near the middle of one side, align the raw edges of the binding with the quilt top. Leaving the first 10" or so of the binding free, stitch the binding to the quilt toward the first corner. End the stitching ¼" from the corner of the quilt and backstitch. Clip the thread.

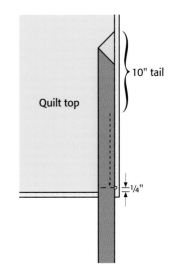

5. Turn the quilt so that you will be stitching down the next side. Fold the binding up, away from the quilt, with the raw edges aligned.

6. Fold the binding back down onto itself, even with the edge of the quilt top. Begin stitching at the corner.

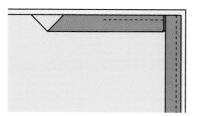

7. Repeat the process on the remaining edges and corners of the quilt. Stop sewing about 15" from where you began. Lay the beginning of the binding flat on the quilt top. Overlap the end of the binding over the beginning. Trim the end so that the overlap measures 2½". (This overlap should be equal to the width of your binding strip.)

2½" overlap

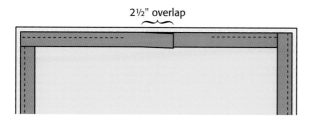

8. Open up the beginning and ending of the binding and place them right sides together at a right angle as shown. Draw a diagonal line and secure the binding with pins.

Pin ends together.
Draw diagonal line.

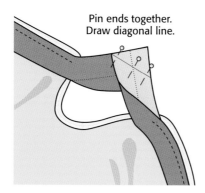

9. Stitch on the diagonal line. Check to make sure you have stitched correctly before trimming the seam allowance to ¼". Press the seam allowance open.

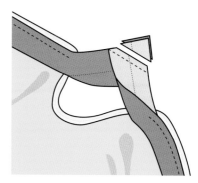

10. Refold the binding in half, laying it flat along the quilt edge. Finish sewing the binding to the top.

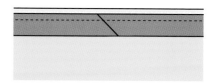

11. Fold the binding over the raw edges of the quilt to the back of the quilt, with the folded edge covering the row of machine stitching. Blindstitch the binding in place. A miter will form at each corner. Blindstitch the mitered corners in place.

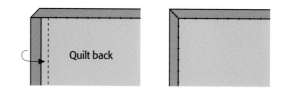

Quilt back

ROUNDED CORNERS

I love to make rounded corners on my quilts. It's so much easier because you do not have to miter the corners. After the quilt is quilted, use a dinner plate as a guide to mark and trim the corners. Make bias binding so that it will ease around the corners nicely.

American Beauty

By Carmen Christian, 2004

Believe it or not, this stunning quilt is made from simple Nine Patch blocks,
put together in an unusual way. The scrappiness really adds to its appeal.

Finished Quilt: 66" x 84"
Finished Block: 9" x 9"

MATERIALS

Yardage is based on 42"-wide fabric.

- 2¼ yards *total* of assorted cream prints, *or* 1 fat quarter *each* of 9 cream prints, for blocks
- 1⅝ yards *total* of assorted black prints, *or* 1 fat quarter *each* of 7 black prints, for blocks
- 1¼ yards *total* of assorted red prints, *or* 1 fat quarter *each* of 5 red prints, for blocks
- 1 yard of black print for outer border
- ⅝ yard of red print for inner border
- ⅝ yard of cream print for middle border
- 5½ yards of fabric for backing
- ¾ yard of fabric for binding
- 70" x 88" piece of batting

CUTTING

From the assorted cream prints, cut a total of:
- 144 squares, 3½" x 3½"
- 48 squares, 4" x 4"

From the assorted red prints, cut a total of:
- 48 squares, 3½" x 3½"
- 48 squares, 4" x 4"

From the assorted black prints, cut a total of:
- 144 squares, 3½" x 3½"

From the red border print, cut:
- 8 strips, 2" x 42"

From the cream border print, cut:
- 8 strips, 2" x 42"

From the black border print, cut:
- 8 strips, 3½" x 42"

From the binding fabric, cut:
- 8 strips, 2½" x 42"

BLOCK ASSEMBLY

1. Referring to "Bias Squares" on page 10, make 96 bias squares. Use the cream and red 4" squares. Trim the bias squares to 3½".

Make 96.

2. Sew together the bias squares made in step 1, and the 3½" black, cream, and red squares as shown, to complete the block. Repeat to make 48 blocks. The blocks should measure 9½" x 9½".

Make 48.

PRESSING FOR SUCCESS

As you sew the rows of the blocks, press the seams of half of them in the opposite direction. Alternate the blocks as you set them together and the seams will butt together perfectly.

QUILT ASSEMBLY

1. Sew the blocks into rows as shown, paying close attention to the orientation of each block. Join the rows.

2. Referring to "Straight-Cut Borders" on page 15, attach the 2"-wide inner and middle borders, and the 3½"-wide outer borders.

3. Layer the quilt top with batting and backing; baste. Quilt as desired.

4. Referring to "Binding" on page 17, bind the edges of the quilt.

Anchors-a-Swirl

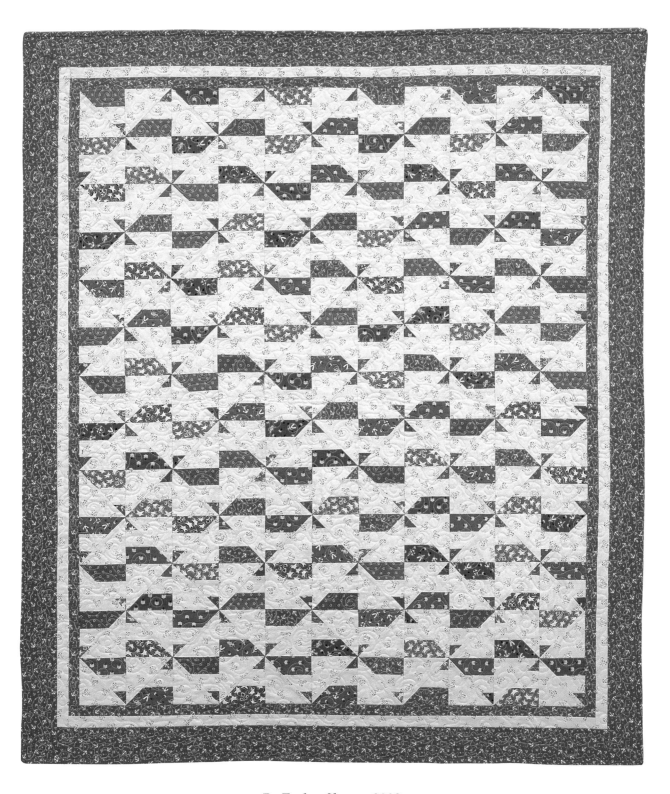

By Evelyn Sloppy, 2003

Looks can be deceiving. Using a fun and easy technique, this nautical-theme quilt is a snap to sew together.
Kids of all ages will love this design.

FINISHED QUILT: 54⅜" x 62⅝"

FINISHED BLOCK: 4⅛" x 4⅛"

MATERIALS

Yardage is based on 42"-wide fabric.

+ 2⅜ yards of background fabric for blocks and middle border
+ 1 yard *total* of assorted red prints, *or* 1 fat quarter *each* of 4 red prints, for blocks
+ 1 yard *total* of assorted blue prints, *or* 1 fat quarter *each* of 4 blue prints, for blocks
+ 1 yard of red print for inner and outer borders
+ 3½ yards of fabric for backing
+ ⅝ yard of fabric for binding
+ 59" x 67" piece of batting

CUTTING

From the assorted red prints, cut a *total* of:

+ 72 pieces, 2" x 5"

From the assorted blue prints, cut a *total* of:

+ 72 pieces, 2" x 5"

From the background fabric, cut:

+ 4 strips, 5" x 42"; crosscut into 72 pieces, 2" x 5"
+ 9 strips, 5" x 42"; crosscut into 72 squares, 5" x 5"
+ 6 strips, 1½" x 42"

From the red print for borders, cut:

+ 6 strips, 1½" x 42"
+ 7 strips, 3" x 42"

From the binding fabric, cut:

+ 7 strips, 2½" x 42"

BLOCK ASSEMBLY

1. Sew three 2" x 5" pieces together along their long edges, with a red piece and a blue piece on the outside, and a background piece in the center. Make 72 of these units. On the wrong side of 36 units, draw a diagonal line from the lower-left corner to the upper-right corner, with the strips in a vertical position. On the remaining 36 units, draw a diagonal line from the upper-left corner to the lower-right corner.

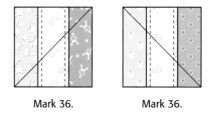

Mark 36.   Mark 36.

2. Place a unit from step 1, right sides together, on top of a 5" x 5" background square. Pin together and stitch a scant ¼" away from both sides of the drawn line. Cut along the drawn line. Repeat with all 72 units. You will have 4 different blocks—36 each of blocks A, B, C, and D as shown. The units should measure 4⅝" x 4⅝".

Block A   Block B
Make 36.   Make 36.

Block C   Block D
Make 36.   Make 36.

QUILT ASSEMBLY

1. Sew the blocks together into rows, as shown, paying close attention to the proper placement of the blocks. You will have one extra block B. Join the rows.

2. Referring to "Straight-Cut Borders" on page 15, add the 1½"-wide red inner border, the 1½"-wide background middle border, and the 3"-wide red outer border.

3. Layer the quilt top with batting and backing; baste. Quilt as desired.

4. Referring to "Binding" on page 17, bind the edges of the quilt.

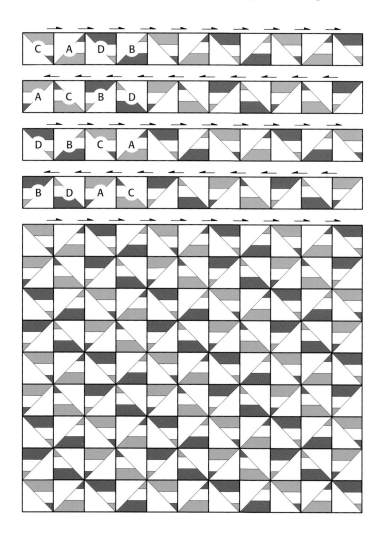

And All That Jazz

By Evelyn Sloppy, 2003

These bright fabrics just reach out and grab you. Three quick and easy blocks make this a cinch to complete in a hurry. This would be a perfect quilt for a family room or college dorm room.

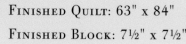

MATERIALS

Yardage is based on 42"-wide fabric.

+ 2⅛ yards of background print for blocks
+ 1⅝ yards of bright blue or green print for blocks and outer border
+ ½ yard *each* of 6 bright blue or green prints for blocks and setting triangles
+ ½ yard of black print for blocks
+ 5⅛ yards of fabric for backing
+ ¾ yard of fabric for binding
+ 67" x 88" piece of batting

CUTTING

From the background print, cut:

+ 7 strips, 3½" x 42"; crosscut into 72 squares, 3½" x 3½"
+ 6 strips, 2" x 42"; crosscut into 18 squares, 2" x 2", and 24 rectangles, 2" x 8"
+ 1 strip, 8" x 42"; crosscut into 1 square, 8" x 8", and 3 squares, 7⅜" x 7⅜". Cut the 7⅜" squares in half once diagonally to make 6 half-square triangles.
+ 1 strip, 7⅜" x 42"; crosscut into 5 squares, 7⅜" x 7⅜". Cut the squares in half once diagonally to make 10 half-square triangles.
+ 7 strips, 2" x 42"

From the assorted bright blue or green prints, cut a *total* of:

+ 5 squares, 12¼" x 12¼". Cut the squares in half twice diagonally to make 20 side setting triangles.*
+ 2 squares, 7" x 7". Cut the squares in half once diagonally to make 4 corner setting triangles.
+ 72 rectangles, 2" x 3½"**
+ 48 rectangles, 3½" x 8"**

+ 8 squares, 7⅜" x 7⅜". Cut the squares in half once diagonally to make 16 half-square triangles.**

Cut the 12¼" squares first, before you cut the other pieces. Otherwise, you may not have a piece large enough to cut the 12¼" squares.
**Include some of the outer-border fabric in the cutting for the blocks. One-half yard has been allowed for this purpose.*

From the bright blue or green print outer-border fabric, cut:

+ 8 strips, 4" x 42"

From the binding fabric, cut:

+ 8 strips, 2½" x 42"

BLOCK ASSEMBLY

1. **Block A:** Sew four 3½" x 3½" background squares, one 2" x 2" background square, and four 2" x 3½" assorted bright print rectangles into rows as shown. Then sew the three rows together to complete block A. The block should measure 8" x 8". Repeat to make 18 blocks.

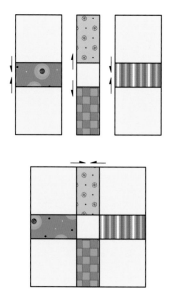

Make 18.

2. **Block B:** Sew together two 3½" x 8" bright print rectangles and one 2" x 8" background piece to complete block B. The block should measure 8" x 8". Make 24 blocks.

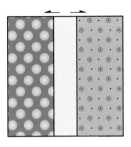

Make 24.

3. **Block C:** Make a template for block C with the pattern on page 29. Trace around the template on the black print fabric and cut 16 pieces. Sew a 7⅜" half-square background triangle to one side of a black print piece, and a 7⅜" half-square bright triangle to the other side. The block should measure 8" x 8". Repeat to make 16 blocks.

Make 16.

QUILT ASSEMBLY

1. Arrange blocks A, B, and C, the 8" x 8" background square, and the bright half-square and quarter-square setting triangles into diagonal rows as shown in the quilt diagram above right. The setting triangles will be slightly oversized. Sew the blocks together in rows.

2. Join the rows. Trim the edges of the quilt as described in "Making Diagonally Set Quilts" on page 14.

3. Referring to "Straight-Cut Borders" on page 15, add the 2"-wide background inner border and the 4"-wide bright blue or green print outer border.

4. Layer the quilt top with batting and backing; baste. Quilt as desired.

5. To make the quilt as shown, with rounded corners, trim the corners using a dinner plate as a guide. Referring to "Binding" on page 17, bind the edges of the quilt. Note that you must use bias binding rather than straight-grain binding if you choose to make rounded corners.

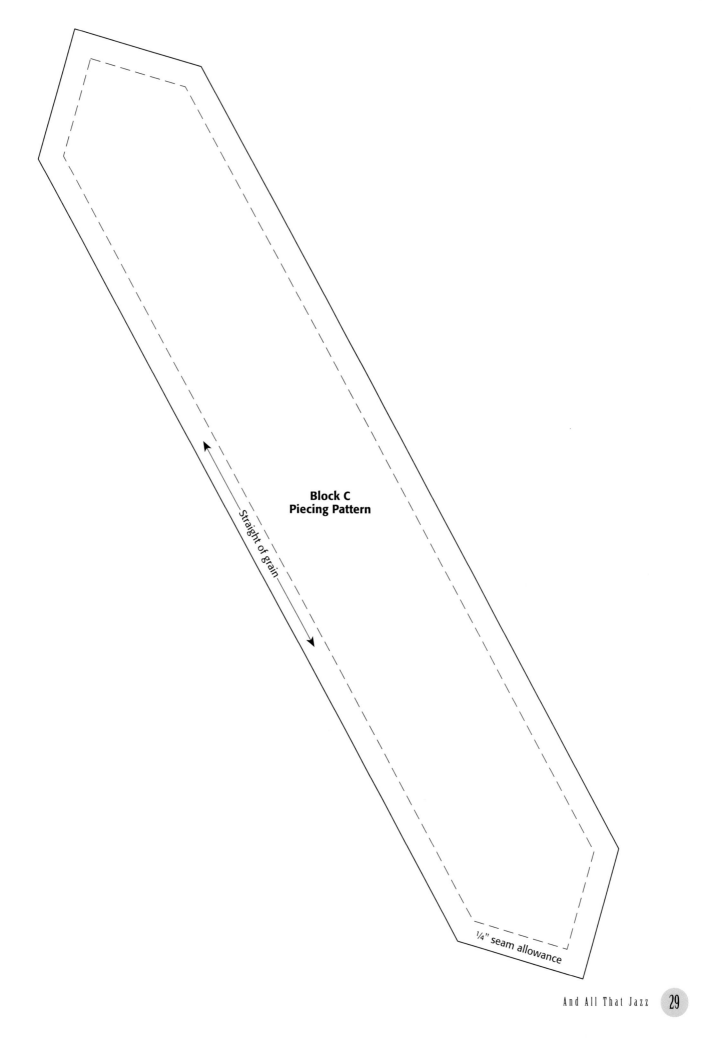

**Block C
Piecing Pattern**

Straight of grain

¼" seam allowance

Anniversary Stars

By Sharon Pennel, 2004

Sharon worked on this warm and inviting quilt while on an anniversary trip with her husband.
The quilt really shows off her talent for selecting fabrics and colors.

MATERIALS

Yardage is based on 42"-wide fabric.

- 3¾ yards *total, or* 15 fat quarters, of assorted light fabrics for blocks
- 2¾ yards *total, or* 11 fat quarters, of assorted dark fabrics for blocks
- 1⅞ yards of print fabric for outer border
- 1 yard *total, or* 4 fat quarters, of assorted reds for the star points
- ¾ yard *total, or* 3 fat quarters, of assorted greens for the star points
- ½ yard of red fabric for inner border
- 5¾ yards of fabric for backing
- ¾ yard of fabric for binding
- 81" x 99" piece of batting

CUTTING

From the assorted reds for the star points, cut a *total* of:

- 40 squares, 4½" x 4½"

From the assorted light fabrics, cut a *total* of:

- 34 strips, 3½" x 21"; crosscut 7 strips into 32 squares, 3½" x 3½"
- 10 strips, 4" x 21"; crosscut into 48 squares, 4" x 4"
- 16 strips, 4½" x 21"; crosscut into 64 squares, 4½" x 4½". Cut 32 squares in half twice diagonally to make 128 triangles.*

From the assorted dark fabrics, cut a *total* of:

- 37 strips, 3½" x 21"; crosscut 7 strips into 32 squares, 3½" x 3½"
- 10 strips, 4" x 21"; crosscut into 48 squares, 4" x 4"

From the assorted greens for the star points, cut a *total* of:

- 24 squares, 4½" x 4½"

From the red fabric for the inner border, cut:

- 8 strips, 1½" x 42"

From the print for the outer border, cut:

- 9 strips, 6½" x 42"

From the binding fabric, cut:

- 9 strips, 2½" x 42"

Before you cut, read the note under "Star Block Assembly" below.

STAR BLOCK ASSEMBLY

Note: Sharon wanted the inner backgrounds of the star-point units in her Star blocks to be the same fabric in each block. The cutting and piecing directions are written so that these fabrics will match. For a scrappy look, you can simply layer two red or green squares and two light squares in step 1 to make four bias squares. Cut them into eight triangles and sew them together as in step 3. If you prefer this simpler approach, do not cut any of the 4½" light squares in half twice diagonally.

1. Using a red 4½" square and a light 4½" square, and referring to "Bias Squares" on page 10, make two bias squares. Do not trim; cut them in half once diagonally to make four triangles.

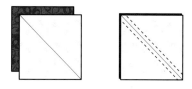

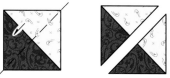

2. Using the same red fabric as you used in step 1, cut a 4½" square in half twice diagonally to make four triangles. Using these red triangles and four assorted light triangles, sew the triangles together along their short sides into pairs as shown. Be sure that the red is on the left side on two pairs and on the right side on the remaining two pairs.

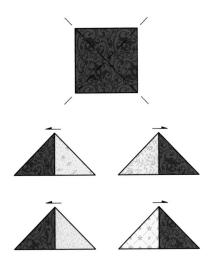

3. Sew together a triangle unit made in step 1 and a triangle unit made in step 2 to make a quarter-square-triangle unit. Make four. Trim to 3½" square. Refer to "Quarter-Square-Triangle Units" on page 11 for trimming instructions.

4. Using the 48 assorted light and 48 assorted dark 4" squares, make 96 bias squares. Trim the bias squares to 3½".

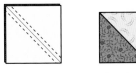

Make 96 total.

5. Using the four quarter-square-triangle units made in steps 1–3, three of the bias squares made in step 4, and one light and one dark 3½" square, assemble the block as shown. The block should measure 9½" x 9½".

6. Repeat steps 1–5 to make 20 blocks with red star points and 12 blocks with green star points.

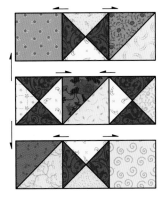

NINE PATCH BLOCK ASSEMBLY

1. Sew together three of the 3½"-wide light strips along their long sides. Make nine strip sets. Crosscut the strip sets into a total of 45 segments, 3½" wide; 30 should be pressed to the inside and 15 should be pressed to the outside. (Press the seams on six strip sets to the inside and press the seams on three strip sets to the outside.)

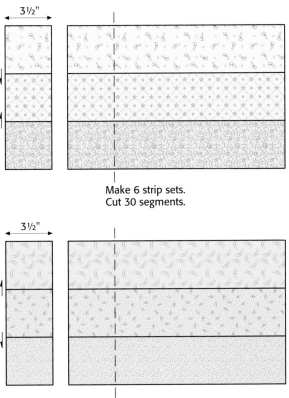

3½"

Make 6 strip sets.
Cut 30 segments.

3½"

Make 3 strip sets.
Cut 15 segments.

2. Sew three segments together to complete a Nine Patch block. The blocks should measure 9½" x 9½". Make 15 blocks.

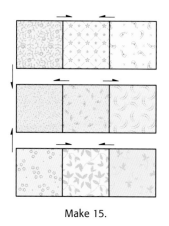

Make 15.

3. Using the 3½"-wide dark strips, make 10 strip sets in the same manner as step 1. Cut a total of 48 segments, 3½" wide; 32 should be pressed to the inside and 16 should be pressed to the outside. Make 16 blocks.

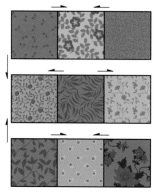

Make 16.

QUILT ASSEMBLY

1. Sew the Star blocks and Nine Patch blocks together into rows, paying close attention to the orientation of the Star blocks. Join the rows.

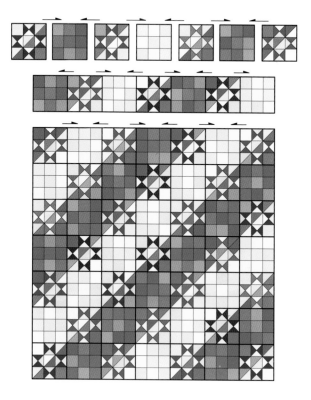

2. Referring to "Straight-Cut Borders" on page 15, attach the 1½"-wide inner border and the 6½"-wide outer border.

3. Layer the quilt top with batting and backing; baste. Quilt as desired.

4. Referring to "Binding" on page 17, bind the edges of the quilt.

Black and Beyond

By Evelyn Sloppy, 2004

When I found a collection of vintage-looking blacks and grays, I just had to have them. Then I had to design a quilt around them, of course! The turkey red print really enhances the vintage look of this quilt.

MATERIALS

Yardage is based on 42"-wide fabric.

◆ 4 yards *total* of light to medium gray prints, *or* 1 fat quarter *each* of 16 light to medium gray prints, for blocks and sashing

◆ 1¾ yards of red print for sashing

◆ 1½ yards *total* of black prints, *or* 1 fat eighth *each* of 12 black prints, for blocks and sashing

◆ 3¾ yards of fabric for backing

◆ ⅝ yard of fabric for binding

◆ 63" x 79" piece of batting

CUTTING

From the gray prints, cut a *total* of:

◆ 40 strips, 1½" x 21"

◆ 2 strips, 2½" x 21"

◆ 26 strips, 3½" x 21"; crosscut 16 of the strips into:

    ◆ 14 rectangles, 3½" x 11½"

    ◆ 18 rectangles, 3½" x 5½"

    ◆ 4 squares, 3½" x 3½"

◆ 22 strips, 4½" x 21"

From the black prints, cut a *total* of:

◆ 59 strips, 1½" x 21"

From the red print, cut:

◆ 3 strips, 5½" x 42"; crosscut into 20 squares, 5½" x 5½"

◆ 13 strips, 3" x 42"; crosscut into 160 squares, 3" x 3"

From the binding fabric, cut:

◆ 7 strips, 2½" x 42"

BLOCK AND SASHING ASSEMBLY

1. Using two gray 2½"-wide strips and one black 1½"-wide strip, sew them together along their long edges as shown. Crosscut the strip sets into 1½"-wide segments. You will need 12 segments.

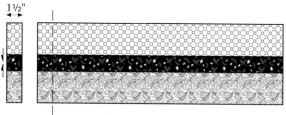

Cut 12 segments.

2. Sew five strips of 1½"-wide black and 1½"-wide gray strips together as shown. Make five strip sets with black strips on the outside and three strip sets with gray strips on the outside. Crosscut the black strip sets into 3½"-wide segments and the gray sets into 2½"-wide segments. You will need 24 segments of each type.

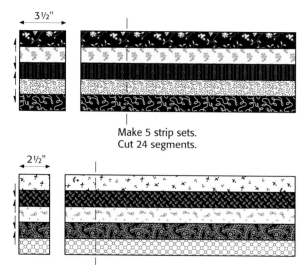

Make 5 strip sets.
Cut 24 segments.

Make 3 strip sets.
Cut 24 segments.

3. Sew together three 1½"-wide black strips, two 1½"-wide gray strips, and two 3½"-wide gray strips as shown. Make five strip sets. Crosscut the strip sets into 3½"-wide segments. You will need 24 segments.

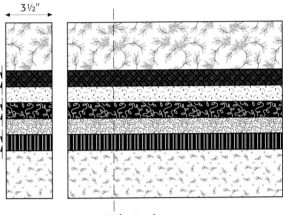

Make 5 strip sets.
Cut 24 segments.

4. Sew one segment made in step 1 and two of the 2½"-wide segments made in step 2 together as shown. Then add two of the 3½"-wide segments made in step 2, and finally two of the segments made in step 3, to complete the block. Repeat to make 12 blocks. They should measure 11½" x 11½".

Make 12.

5. Sew two gray 4½"-wide strips, two black 1½"-wide strips, and one gray 1½"-wide strip together as shown. Make 11 strip sets. Crosscut the strip sets into 5½"-wide segments. You will need 31 segments.

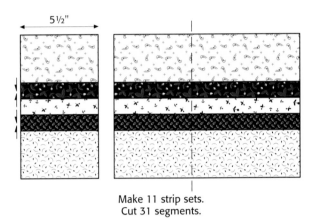

Make 11 strip sets.
Cut 31 segments.

6. Draw a diagonal line on the wrong side of the 3" red squares. Referring to "Folded Corners" on page 12, sew a red square on all four corners of each unit made in step 5.

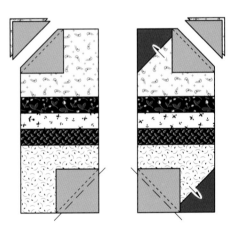

Make 31.

QUILT ASSEMBLY

1. Sew the blocks, sashing units, and 5½" red squares together into rows as shown. Join the rows.

2. Referring to "Folded Corners" on page 12, sew a red square on two corners of a 3½" x 5½" gray rectangle. Repeat to make 18 blocks.

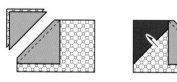

Make 18.

3. Sew five blocks made in step 2 and four gray 3½" x 11½" rectangles together for each side border. Then sew four blocks from step 2 and three gray 3½" x 11½" rectangles together for the top and bottom borders, and attach a 3½" gray square to both ends. Sew the side borders to the quilt first, and then add the top and bottom borders.

4. Layer the quilt with batting and backing; baste. Quilt as desired.

5. Referring to "Binding" on page 17, bind the edges of the quilt.

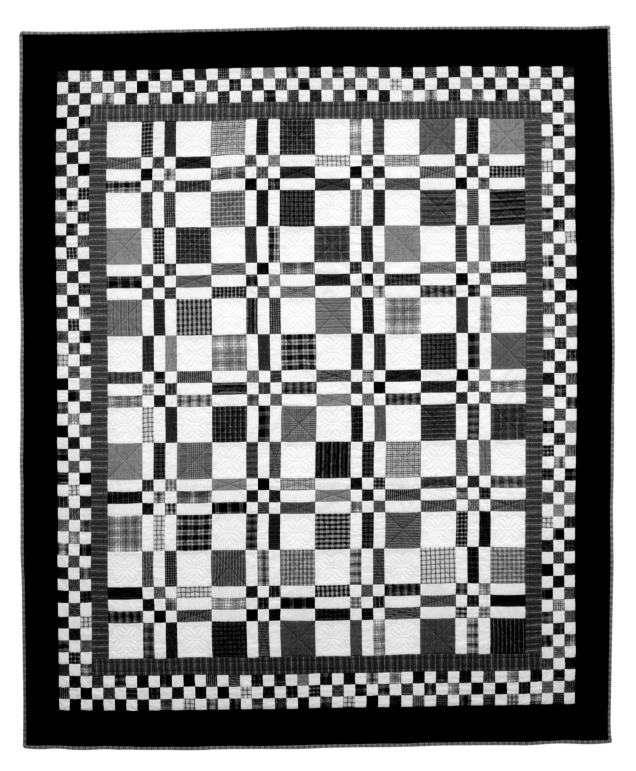

By Evelyn Sloppy, 2003

What could be more earthy and appealing than plaid flannels or homespuns paired with muslin?
This is a great comfort quilt. It just begs to be used.

MATERIALS

Yardage is based on 42"-wide fabric.

+ 3¼ yards *total*, *or* 12 to 15 fat quarters, of assorted plaid and stripe flannels, or homespuns for blocks and middle border
+ 3 yards of good-quality muslin for blocks and middle border
+ 1½ yards of plaid for outer border
+ ¾ yard of plaid for inner border
+ 5½ yards of fabric for backing
+ ¾ yard of fabric for binding
+ 80" x 94" piece of batting

CUTTING

From the assorted flannels or homespuns, cut a *total* of:

+ 40 squares, 5" x 5"
+ 69 strips, 2" x 21"

From the muslin, cut:

+ 5 strips, 5" x 42"; crosscut into 40 squares, 5" x 5"
+ 35 strips, 2" x 42"; cut each strip in half to make 70 strips, 2" x 21"

From the plaid for the inner border, cut:

+ 7 strips, 2¾" x 42"

From the plaid for the outer border, cut:

+ 9 strips, 5" x 42"

From the binding fabric, cut:

+ 9 strips, 2½" x 42"

BLOCK ASSEMBLY

1. Sew the assorted 2"-wide plaid and muslin strips into strip sets as shown. Crosscut the strip sets into 2"-wide segments. You will need 123 of the 2" segments from each type of strip set.

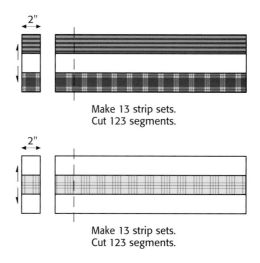

Make 13 strip sets.
Cut 123 segments.

Make 13 strip sets.
Cut 123 segments.

2. Sew the 2" segments together to make the two types of nine-patch units. You will need 41 of each type of nine-patch unit. These units will be used in the blocks and the middle border. The units should measure 5" x 5".

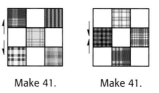

Make 41.   Make 41.

3. Sew the assorted 2"-wide plaid and muslin strips together into strip sets as shown. Crosscut the strip sets into 5"-wide segments. You will need 40 segments from each type of strip set.

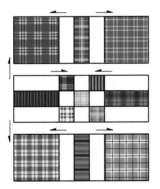

Make 10 strip sets.
Cut 40 segments.

Make 10 strip sets.
Cut 40 segments.

4. Sew the assorted plaid and muslin 5" squares, the nine-patch units made in step 2, and the segments made in step 3 together into rows as shown. Then sew the rows together to complete block A and block B. They should measure 14" x 14". Make 10 of each block.

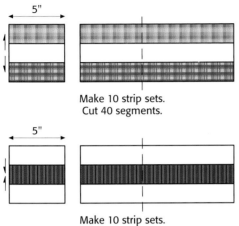

Block A
Make 10.

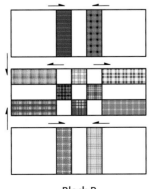

Block B
Make 10.

QUILT ASSEMBLY

1. Sew the blocks together into rows, alternating block A and block B. Join the rows.

2. Referring to "Straight-Cut Borders" on page 15, add the 2¾"-wide inner border.

3. Sew together 16 nine-patch units to make the middle border for each side. Alternate the type of nine-patch unit so that you make a checkerboard design. Attach the side borders. Sew together 15 nine-patch units for the top and bottom middle borders. Attach these to complete the middle border.

4. Add the 5"-wide outer border.

5. Layer the quilt top with batting and backing; baste. Quilt as desired.

6. Referring to "Binding" on page 17, bind the edges of the quilt.

Cheerio

By Evelyn Sloppy, 2003

This bright and cheery quilt is ideal for using scraps or fat quarters. It will provide the opportunity for plenty of practice in making bias squares and quarter-square-triangle units—the easy way, of course!

FINISHED QUILT: 68" x 84"
FINISHED BLOCK: 8" x 8"

MATERIALS

Yardage is based on 42"-wide fabric.

- 3 yards *total, or* 12 fat quarters, of assorted yellow or cream prints for blocks and middle border
- 2 yards *total, or* 8 fat quarters, of assorted blue prints for blocks and middle border
- 1¾ yards of blue print for inner and outer borders
- 1 yard *total, or* 4 fat quarters, of assorted red prints for blocks and middle border
- 1 yard *total, or* 4 fat quarters, of assorted green prints for blocks and middle border
- 5⅛ yards of fabric for backing
- ¾ yard of fabric for binding
- 72" x 88" piece of batting

CUTTING

From the assorted blue prints, cut a *total* of:
- 48 squares, 5" x 5"
- 96 squares, 2½" x 2½"
- 16 squares, 5½" x 5½"

From the assorted yellow or cream prints, cut a *total* of:
- 48 squares, 5" x 5"
- 96 squares, 2½" x 2½"
- 96 squares, 3" x 3"
- 32 squares, 5½" x 5½"

From the assorted red prints, cut a *total* of:
- 48 squares, 3" x 3"
- 8 squares, 5½" x 5½"

From the assorted green prints, cut a *total* of:
- 48 squares, 3" x 3"
- 8 squares, 5½" x 5½"

From the blue print for borders, cut:
- 7 strips, 2½" x 42"
- 8 strips, 4½" x 42"

From the binding fabric, cut:
- 8 strips, 2½" x 42"

BLOCK ASSEMBLY

1. Referring to "Bias Squares" on page 10, make 96 bias squares with the 5" blue squares and the 5" yellow or cream squares. Trim the bias squares to 4½".

Make 96.

2. In the same manner as step 1, make 96 bias squares with the 3" red squares and the 3" yellow or cream squares. Also make 96 bias squares with the 3" green squares and the 3" yellow or cream squares. Trim the bias squares to 2½".

Make 96.

Make 96.

3. Sew the units together for the block as shown. Each block requires two large bias squares made in step 1, two small bias squares of both the green and the red prints made in step 2, two blue 2½" squares, and two yellow or cream 2½" squares. Make 48 blocks. The blocks should measure 8½" x 8½".

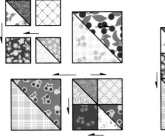
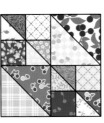

Make 48.

QUILT ASSEMBLY

1. Sew the blocks into rows as shown, being sure to alternate the direction of the blocks. Join the rows.

2. Referring to "Straight-Cut Borders" on page 15, attach the 2½"-wide inner borders.

3. Referring to "Quarter-Square-Triangle Units" on page 11, and using the assorted blue, red, green, and cream 5½" squares, make 64 quarter-square-triangle units. Trim the units to 4½". Pair a yellow or cream square with a blue, red, or green square.

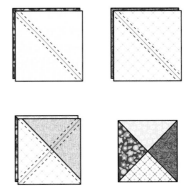

Make 64 total.

4. Sew 17 of the units together, alternating the direction of each unit, for the side border. Repeat and attach to each side of the quilt. Sew 15 units together for the top and bottom borders and attach them to the quilt.

5. Attach the 4½"-wide outer borders.

6. Layer the quilt top with batting and backing; baste. Quilt as desired.

7. Referring to "Binding" on page 17, bind the edges of the quilt.

Cherry Spinners

By Evelyn Sloppy, 2001

Try this easy sewing trick, and half your Pinwheel blocks spin in one direction and the other half spin in the opposite direction. The different prints blend together beautifully to make this romantic quilt that any girl would adore.

MATERIALS

Yardage is based on 42"-wide fabric.

- 1⅜ yards of small-scale yellow print for blocks and sashings
- 1⅜ yards of green print for blocks and setting triangles
- Scraps of 4 to 6 assorted red prints, *or* a *total* of ⅝ yard of red prints, for blocks
- Scraps of 4 to 6 assorted green prints, *or* a *total* of ½ yard of green prints, for blocks
- ⅜ yard of large-scale yellow print for blocks
- 2¾ yards of fabric for backing
- ⅝ yard of fabric for binding
- 44" x 61" piece of batting

CUTTING

From the assorted green prints, cut a *total* of:
- 34 squares, 3½" x 3½"

From the small-scale yellow print, cut:
- 4 strips, 3½" x 42"; crosscut into 34 squares, 3½" x 3½"
- 3 strips, 8½" x 42"; crosscut into 24 rectangles, 4½" x 8½"

From the assorted red prints, cut a *total* of:
- 68 squares, 3" x 3"

From the large-scale yellow print, cut:
- 2 strips, 3¾" x 42"; crosscut into 16 squares, 3¾" x 3¾". Cut the squares in half once diagonally to make 32 triangles.

From the 1⅜ yards of green print, cut:
- 2 strips, 4⅞" x 42"; crosscut into 16 squares, 4⅞" x 4⅞". Cut the squares in half once diagonally to make 32 triangles.
- 2 squares, 19" x 19"; cut the squares in half twice diagonally to make 8 side setting triangles. You will have 2 left over.

- 2 squares, 12½" x 12½"; cut the squares in half once diagonally to make 4 corner setting triangles

From the binding fabric, cut:
- 6 strips, 2½" x 42"

BLOCK ASSEMBLY

1. To make the pinwheel units, you will need two 3½" squares of one green print, two 3½" squares of the small yellow print, and four 3" squares of one red print. Referring to "Bias Squares" on page 10, make four bias squares with the 3½" green and yellow squares. Do not trim.

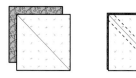

Make 4.

2. Draw a diagonal line on the wrong side of the bias squares made in step 1. Place a bias square on a 3" red square, right sides together. Stitch ¼" from both sides of the drawn line. Cut on the drawn line and press the units. Trim to 2½" square. You will have two different units, four of each.

Trim to 2½".

3. Sew four like units made in step 2 together to make a pinwheel unit. Sew the other four units together to make another pinwheel unit. One unit will spin to the right; the other one will

spin to the left. Repeat steps 1 through 3 to make 34 pinwheel units, 17 that spin to the right and 17 that spin to the left.

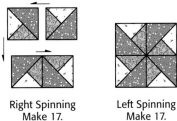

Right Spinning
Make 17.

Left Spinning
Make 17.

4. Set aside the right-spinning pinwheel units. These will be used as cornerstones when assembling the quilt. Pick eight of the left-spinning pinwheel units to use in the Pinwheel blocks. The remaining nine units are extra; put them on the back of your quilt or save them for another project.

5. For each Pinwheel block, you will need a left-spinning pinwheel unit, four yellow print triangles cut from the 3¾" squares, and four green print triangles cut from the 4⅞" squares. Sew two yellow triangles to opposite sides of the pinwheel unit.

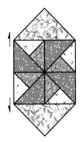

6. Sew the remaining two yellow triangles to the remaining sides.

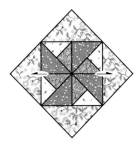

7. In the same manner as steps 5 and 6, add the green triangles. Your block should measure 8½" x 8½". Repeat to make eight blocks.

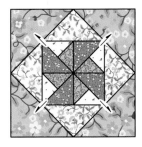

Make 8.

QUILT ASSEMBLY

1. Sew the eight Pinwheel blocks, 17 right-spinning pinwheel units, the 4½" x 8½" yellow print sashing strips, and the green side and corner setting triangles together into diagonal rows as shown. Join the rows. Trim the edges of the quilt as described in "Making Diagonally Set Quilts" on page 14.

2. Layer the quilt top with batting and backing; baste. Quilt as desired.

3. Referring to "Binding" on page 17, bind the edges of the quilt.

By Evelyn Sloppy, 2003

These solid colors make a bright, cheery quilt for a child. What a fun way for a child to learn colors!
Older kids will surely appreciate the bold graphic design as well.

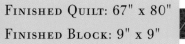
MATERIALS

Yardage is based on 42"-wide fabric.

- ✦ 2 yards of yellow fabric for blocks and setting triangles
- ✦ 1¼ yards of green fabric for blocks and borders
- ✦ 1¼ yards of purple fabric for blocks and borders
- ✦ 1⅛ yards of black fabric for blocks
- ✦ 1 yard of blue fabric for blocks and borders
- ✦ 1 yard of red fabric for blocks and borders
- ✦ 4⅞ yards of fabric for backing
- ✦ ¾ yard of fabric for binding
- ✦ 71" x 84" piece of batting

CUTTING

From the yellow fabric, cut:

- ✦ 4 strips, 5½" x 42"; crosscut into 24 squares, 5½" x 5½"
- ✦ 3 strips, 3½" x 42"; crosscut into 32 squares, 3½" x 3½"
- ✦ 4 squares, 14½" x 14½"; cut the squares in half twice diagonally to make 16 side setting triangles. You will have 2 left over.
- ✦ 2 squares, 8" x 8"; cut the squares in half once diagonally to make 4 corner setting triangles.

From the green fabric, cut:

- ✦ 2 strips, 5½" x 42"; crosscut into 8 squares, 5½" x 5½"
- ✦ 2 strips, 3½" x 42"; crosscut into 16 squares, 3½" x 3½"
- ✦ 8 strips, 2½" x 42"

From the purple fabric, cut:

- ✦ 2 strips, 5½" x 42"; crosscut into 8 squares, 5½" x 5½"
- ✦ 2 strips, 3½" x 42"; crosscut into 16 squares, 3½" x 3½"
- ✦ 8 strips, 2½" x 42"

From the blue fabric, cut:

- ✦ 1 strip, 5½" x 42"; crosscut into 4 squares, 5½" x 5½"
- ✦ 1 strip, 3½" x 42"; crosscut into 8 squares, 3½" x 3½"
- ✦ 8 strips, 2½" x 42"

From the red fabric, cut:

- ✦ 1 strip, 5½" x 42"; crosscut into 4 squares, 5½" x 5½"
- ✦ 1 strip, 3½" x 42"; crosscut into 8 squares, 3½" x 3½"
- ✦ 8 strips, 2½" x 42"

From the black fabric, cut:

- ✦ 10 strips, 3½" x 42"; crosscut into 100 squares, 3½" x 3½"

From the binding fabric, cut:

- ✦ 8 strips, 2½" x 42"

BLOCK ASSEMBLY

1. Referring to "Bias Squares" on page 10, make 16 bias squares with eight yellow and eight green 5½" squares. Trim the bias squares to 5".

Make 16.

2. Sew four bias squares together for the Pinwheel block as shown. Repeat to make four blocks. The blocks should measure 9½" x 9½".

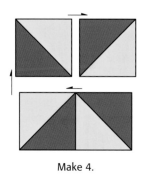

Make 4.

3. Repeat steps 1 and 2 to make four purple, two blue, and two red Pinwheel blocks.

4. Sew the 3½" squares together into rows and blocks as shown. The Nine Patch blocks should measure 9½" x 9½".

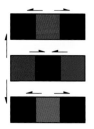

Make 3.   Make 3.

Make 3.   Make 2.   Make 2.

Make 1.   Make 1.   Make 1.

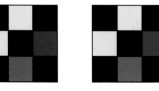

Make 3.   Make 1.

QUILT ASSEMBLY

1. Sew the blocks and setting triangles together into diagonal rows as shown. Refer to "Making Diagonally Set Quilts" on page 14 to trim and square up the quilt top.

2. Referring to "Mitered Borders" on page 16, attach the 2½"-wide borders. Notice that the order of the border colors is different on each side of the quilt.

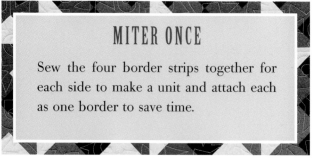

MITER ONCE

Sew the four border strips together for each side to make a unit and attach each as one border to save time.

3. Layer the quilt top with batting and backing; baste. Quilt as desired.

4. Referring to "Binding" on page 17, bind the edges of the quilt.

Deep Blue Sea

By Evelyn Sloppy, 2003

The cool blues and greens in this quilt have a very relaxing, calming effect on the eyes.
The block is actually a Log Cabin, with lots of folded corners and lots of fun, too!

 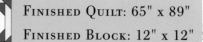
MATERIALS

Yardage is based on 42"-wide fabric.

- 4½ yards *total, or* 9 half yards, of assorted light blues *or* greens for blocks and border
- 4⅜ yards of blue fabric for blocks and borders
- 5½ yards of fabric for backing
- ¾ yard of fabric for binding (or use leftover light blue and green scraps for a scrappy binding)
- 69" x 93" piece of batting

CUTTING

From the blue fabric, cut:

- 6 strips, 2½" x 42"; crosscut into 96 squares, 2½" x 2½"
- 18 strips, 3½" x 42"; crosscut into 192 squares, 3½" x 3½"
- 7 strips, 3½" x 42"
- 8 strips, 4½" x 42"

From the assorted light blue or green fabrics, choose 2 fabrics for each of the 24 blocks.

- **From one of the chosen fabrics, cut the following for each block:**
    - 1 square, 6½" x 6½"
    - 2 strips, 2" x 9½"
    - 2 strips, 2" x 12½"
- **From the second chosen fabric, cut the following for each block:**
    - 2 strips, 2" x 6½"
    - 2 strips, 2" x 9½"

From the binding fabric, cut:

- 8 strips, 2½" x 42"

BLOCK ASSEMBLY

1. Draw a diagonal line on the back of all the 2½" and 3½" blue squares.

2. Using the two light blue or green fabrics you chose and cut for one block, sew 2½" blue squares from step 1 on all four corners of a light blue or green 6½" square; refer to "Folded Corners" on page 12. Stitch on the drawn diagonal line and trim ¼" from the stitching line.

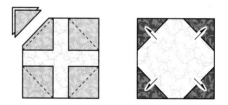

3. Sew two 2" x 6½" light blue or green strips on the opposite sides of your unit from step 2. Then sew two 2" x 9½" strips to the two remaining sides.

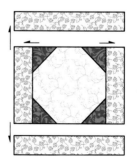

4. Using the same technique for folded corners, sew a 3½" blue square to all four corners of the unit and trim.

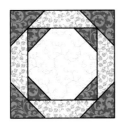

5. Using the same fabric as the center square, sew two 2" x 9½" strips on the opposite sides of your unit. Then sew two 2" x 12½" strips to the two remaining sides. Sew a 3½" blue square to all four corners of the unit as you did in step 4.

6. Repeat steps 1–5 to make 24 blocks. The blocks should measure 12½" x 12½".

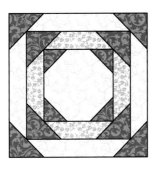

Make 24.

QUILT ASSEMBLY

1. Sew the blocks together into rows as shown. Join the rows.

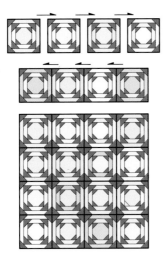

2. Referring to "Straight-Cut Borders" on page 15, attach the 3½"-wide blue inner border.

3. From the remaining light blues and greens, cut 2"-wide strips of varying lengths, anywhere from 2" to 8". Sew the strips together to obtain the necessary lengths for the middle borders and attach them to the quilt top.

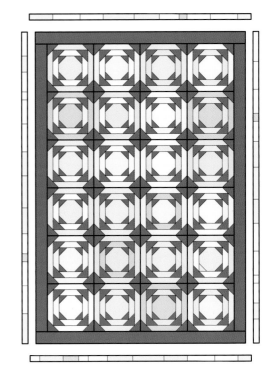

4. Attach the 4½"-wide blue outer border.

5. Layer the quilt top with batting and backing; baste. Quilt as desired.

6. Referring to "Binding" on page 17, bind the edges of the quilt. To make a scrappy binding as shown on this quilt, cut 2½"-wide strips of varying lengths and sew them together to obtain the necessary length.

Down the Garden Path

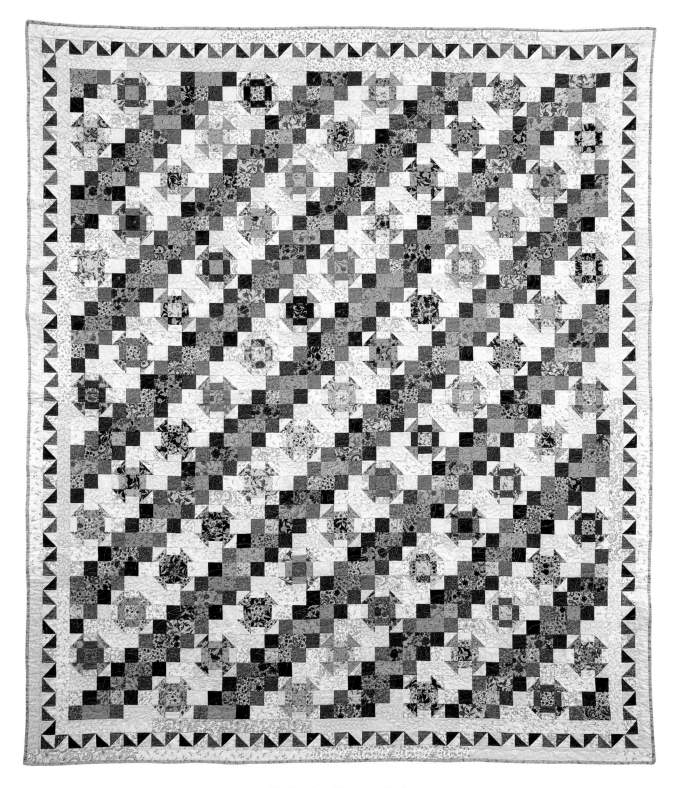

By Evelyn Sloppy, 2001
*If you want to use up lots of scraps, here's the quilt for you. Or simply use a collection
of fabrics that you love, with a good variety of lights, mediums, and darks.*

MATERIALS

Yardage is based on 42"-wide fabric.

- 5⅞ yards *total* of assorted light fabrics, *or* 1 yard *each* of 6 light fabrics, for blocks and border
- 3¾ yards *total* of assorted dark fabrics, *or* ½ yard *each* of 8 dark fabrics, for blocks and border
- 3 yards *total* of assorted medium fabrics, *or* ½ yard *each* of 6 medium fabrics, for blocks
- 8¼ yards of fabric for backing
- ⅞ yard of fabric for binding
- 94" x 106" piece of batting

CUTTING

From the assorted light fabrics, cut a *total* of:

- 17 strips, 3" x 42"; crosscut into 220 squares, 3" x 3"
- 17 strips, 1½" x 42"
- 29 strips, 2½" x 42"
- 9 strips, 4½" x 42"

From the assorted medium and dark fabrics, cut a *total* of:

- 65 squares, 2½" x 2½"
- 17 strips, 1½" x 42"
- 10 strips, 3" x 42"; crosscut into 130 squares, 3" x 3"

From the assorted dark fabrics, cut a *total* of:

- 27 strips, 2½" x 42"
- 7 strips, 3" x 42"; crosscut into 90 squares, 3" x 3"

From the assorted medium fabrics, cut a *total* of:

- 9 strips, 2½" x 42"
- 9 strips, 4½" x 42"

From the binding fabric, cut:

- 10 strips, 2½" x 42"

CHURN DASH BLOCK ASSEMBLY

1. For each block, choose two light fabrics and three medium or dark fabrics as shown.

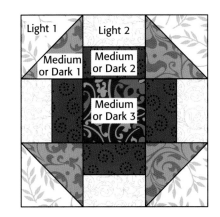

2. Referring to "Bias Squares" on page 10, make four bias squares with 3" squares of light and medium or dark fabrics. Trim the bias squares to 2½".

Make 4.

3. Sew the light and medium or dark 1½"-wide strips together along their long edges. Crosscut the strip set into four 2½"-wide segments. Save the rest of the strip set for another block.

2½"

Cut 4 segments.

4. Sew the segments and bias squares together into three rows, including a dark or medium 2½" square. Sew the rows together. The blocks should measure 6½" x 6½".

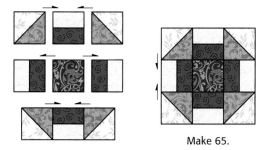

Make 65.

5. Repeat steps 1–4 to make 65 Churn Dash blocks.

CHAIN BLOCK ASSEMBLY

1. Sew a dark 2½"-wide strip and a light 4½"-wide strip together along their long edges. Crosscut the strip set into 2½"-wide segments. Repeat with other dark and light fabrics to make a total of nine strip sets cut into 130 segments.

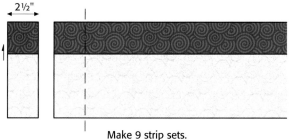

2½"

Make 9 strip sets.
Cut 130 segments.

2. Sew a medium, a dark, and a light 2½"-wide strip together along their long edges, with the dark strip in the middle. Crosscut the strip set into 2½"-wide segments. Repeat with the other light, medium, and dark fabrics to make a total of nine strip sets cut into 130 segments.

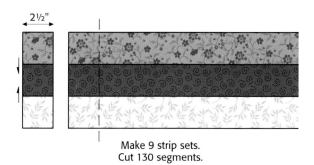

2½"

Make 9 strip sets.
Cut 130 segments.

3. Sew a dark 2½"-wide strip and a medium 4½"-wide strip together along their long edges. Crosscut the strip set into 2½"-wide segments. Repeat with other dark and medium fabrics to make a total of nine strip sets cut into 130 segments.

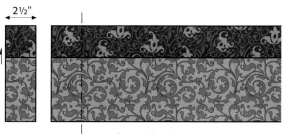

2½"

Make 9 strip sets.
Cut 130 segments.

4. Sew one of each segment from steps 1, 2, and 3 together to make the chain block. Repeat to make 130 blocks. The blocks should measure 6½" x 6½".

Make 130.

QUILT ASSEMBLY

1. Sew the blocks together into rows as shown. Join the rows.

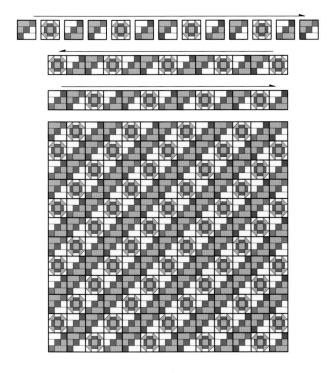

2. Cut the remaining 2½"-wide light strips into varying lengths of anywhere from 10" to 20". Sew them together to obtain the necessary lengths for the inner border. Referring to "Straight-Cut Borders" on page 15, attach the inner border.

3. From the remaining light and dark 3" squares, make 180 bias squares. Trim to 2½" square. Sew these together as shown to make two borders of 47 bias squares each for the sides and two borders of 43 bias squares each for the top and bottom. Attach the two side borders, and then attach the top and bottom border.

4. Sew the rest of the 2½"-wide light strips of varying lengths together to obtain the necessary lengths for the outer border. Attach the outer borders.

5. Layer the quilt top with batting and backing; baste. Quilt as desired.

6. Referring to "Binding" on page 17, bind the edges of the quilt.

Elegant Garden

By Robin Bray, 2004

*Working with these fabrics was out of Robin's comfort zone, but she grew to love them
and she plans to use this quilt for Christmas decorating. Strip piecing makes the blocks a breeze.*

MATERIALS

Yardage is based on 42"-wide fabric.

- 2 yards of red print for setting triangles and outer border
- 1⅛ yards of cream print for blocks and sashing
- 1 yard *total* of assorted green prints, *or* 1 fat quarter *each* of 4 green prints, for blocks
- 1 yard *total* of assorted red prints, *or* 1 fat quarter *each* of 4 red prints, for blocks
- ⅝ yard of blue print for blocks and sashing corner squares
- ½ yard of cream print for inner border
- ½ yard of green print for middle border
- 4 yards of fabric for backing
- ⅝ yard of fabric for binding
- 69" x 69" piece of batting

CUTTING

From the assorted red prints, cut a *total* of:
- 12 strips, 3½" x 21"

From the assorted green prints, cut a *total* of:
- 15 strips, 2" x 21"
- 6 strips, 3½" x 21"

From the cream print, cut:
- 6 strips, 5" x 42"
- 3 strips, 2" x 42"; cut each strip in half to make 6 strips, 2" x 21"

From the blue print, cut:
- 8 strips, 2" x 42"; crosscut 2 of the strips into 24 squares, 2" x 2". Cut 3 strips in half to make 6 strips, 2" x 21".

From the red print for the setting triangles and outer border, cut:
- 2 squares, 18½" x 18½"; cut the squares in half twice diagonally to make 8 side setting triangles
- 2 squares, 10½" x 10½"; cut the squares in half once diagonally to make 4 corner setting triangles
- 7 strips, 4½" x 42"

From the cream print for the inner border, cut:
- 6 strips, 2" x 42"

From the green print for the middle border, cut:
- 6 strips, 2" x 42"

From the binding fabric, cut:
- 7 strips, 2½" x 42"

BLOCK ASSEMBLY

1. Sew two red 3½" x 21" strips, two green 2" x 21" strips, and one cream 2" x 21" strip together along the long edges as shown. Make six of these strip sets. Crosscut the strip sets into 3½"-wide segments. You will need 26 segments.

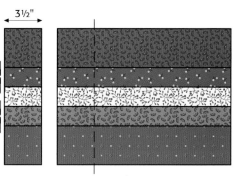

Make 6 strip sets.
Cut 26 segments.

2. Sew two green 3½" x 21" strips, two blue 2" x 21" strips, and one green 2" x 21" strip together along the long edges as shown. Make three of these strip sets. Crosscut the strip sets into 2"-wide segments. You will need 26 segments.

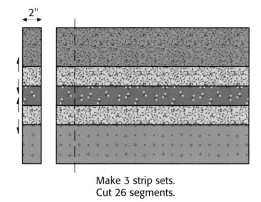

Make 3 strip sets.
Cut 26 segments.

3. Sew two cream 5" x 42" strips and one blue 2" x 42" strip together along the long edges as shown. Make three of these strip sets. For the sashing, press the seam allowances of two strip sets toward the blue. Crosscut the strip sets into 36 segments, 2" wide. For the blocks, press the seams of the remaining strip set away from the blue. Crosscut the strip set into 13 segments, 2" wide.

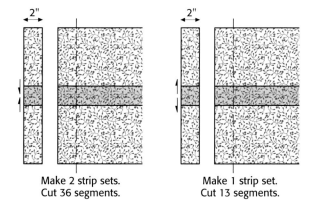

Make 2 strip sets.   Make 1 strip set.
Cut 36 segments.   Cut 13 segments.

4. Sew two segments made in step 1, two segments made in step 2, and one block segment made in step 3 (pressed away from the blue) together

to complete the block. It should measure 11" x 11". Repeat to make 13 blocks.

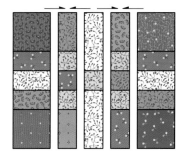

Make 13.

QUILT ASSEMBLY

1. Sew the blocks, sashing strips, 2" blue squares, and setting triangles together into diagonal rows as shown. The side and corner setting triangles will be slightly oversized. Join the rows. Trim the edges of the quilt as described in "Making Diagonally Set Quilts" on page 14. You can trim so that the outer sashing squares become triangles, which was done for the quilt in the photograph on page 57, or you can trim and keep them as squares.

2. Referring to "Straight-Cut Borders" on page 15, add the 2"-wide cream print inner border, 2"-wide green print middle border, and 4½"-wide red print outer border.

3. Layer the quilt top with batting and backing; baste. Quilt as desired.

4. Referring to "Binding" on page 17, bind the edges of the quilt.

Entwined

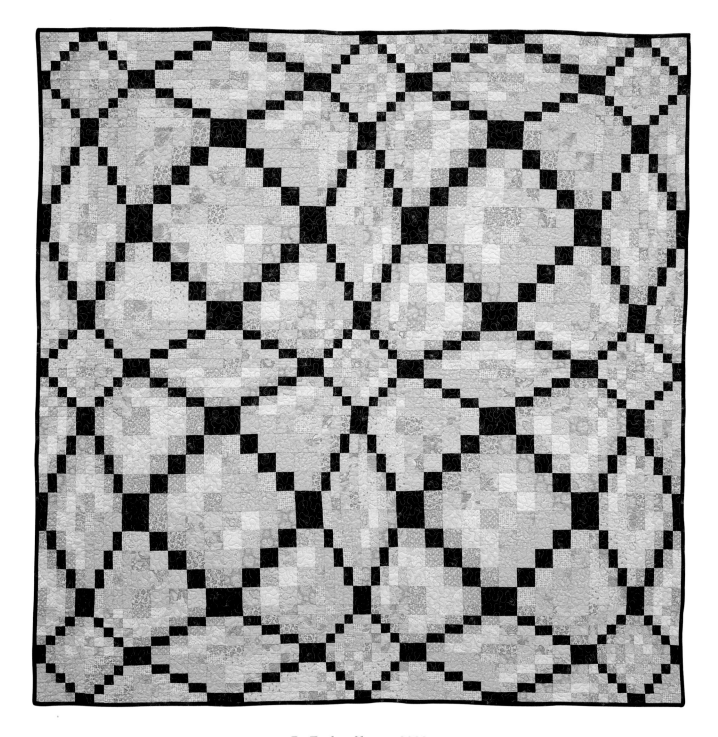

By Evelyn Sloppy, 2003

It's hard to pick out the blocks in this quilt; they just blend together.
You'll never believe how easily this complex-looking quilt goes together. Strip piecing makes it fast and fun.

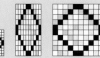
MATERIALS

Yardage is based on 42"-wide fabric.

- ✦ 1⅝ yards of blue print for blocks
- ✦ ½ yard *each* of 14 neutral background prints for blocks
- ✦ 4⅜ yards of fabric for backing
- ✦ ¾ yard of fabric for binding
- ✦ 74" x 74" piece of batting

CUTTING

From the blue print, cut:

- ✦ 15 strips, 2½" x 42"
- ✦ 8 strips, 1½" x 42"

From the assorted background prints, cut:

- ✦ 60 strips, 2½" x 42"
- ✦ 32 strips, 1½" x 42"

From the binding fabric, cut:

- ✦ 8 strips, 2½" x 42"

BLOCK ASSEMBLY

1. Sew one blue and four background 2½"-wide strips together along their long edges. Press. Number the background fabrics 1–4 as shown.

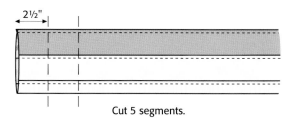

2. Bring the outside strips right sides together and sew along their long edges to make a tube. Crosscut five 2½"-wide segments from the tube. Make sure the tube lies flat and straight before cutting.

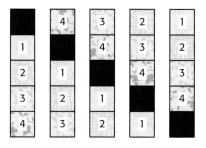

Cut 5 segments.

3. Remove the stitching between the blue and fabric 4 on one segment. On the next segment, remove the stitching between fabrics 3 and 4. Remove the stitching between fabrics 2 and 3 on the third segment, between fabrics 1 and 2 on the fourth segment, and between the blue and fabric 1 on the fifth segment as shown.

4. Sew these five segments together, matching seams. Re-press the seams on the second and fourth segments in the opposite direction so that all the seams butt together properly as you sew the segments together. The unit should measure 10½" x 10½".

5. Repeat steps 1–4 with the rest of the tube and with other combinations of background fabrics. Make four more strip sets (tubes) and cut 75

additional segments (for a total of 80). You will make 16 of these units. On 8 of the units, make the blue travel from the upper left to the lower right. On the other 8, make the blue travel from the lower left to the upper right.

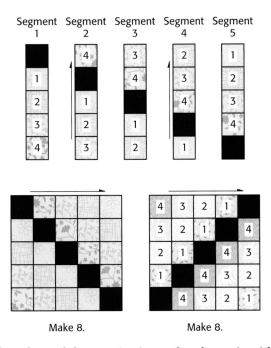

Make 8. Make 8.

6. Sew four of these units (two of each type), with varying background fabrics, together as shown to make a block. The blocks should measure 20½" x 20½". Make four blocks. Follow the pressing arrows in the diagrams and you will be able to butt the seam allowances together when making the blocks and assembling the quilt. Rotate the units and blocks as needed, and your seams will all butt together properly.

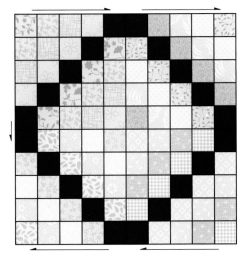

Make 4.

SASHING BLOCK ASSEMBLY

Follow steps 1–6 under "Block Assembly on pages 61–62," but crosscut the strip sets (tubes) into five 1½"-wide segments instead of 2½". Make a total of 10 strip sets. Cut 240 segments to make 48 units, and then sew 4 of these units together to make a sashing block. They should measure 10½" x 20½". Make 12 blocks.

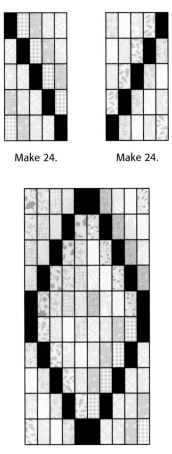

Make 24. Make 24.

Make 12.

CORNERSTONE BLOCK ASSEMBLY

For the cornerstone blocks, assemble eight strip sets with the 1½"-wide blue and background print strips. As described in steps 1–6 of "Block Assembly," make tubes with the strip sets and crosscut the tubes into 1½"-wide segments. Cut 180 segments to make a total of 36 units, and then sew 4 units together to make a cornerstone block. It should measure 10½" x 10½". Make nine cornerstone blocks.

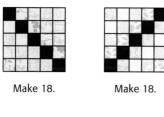

Make 18.　　Make 18.

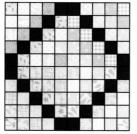

Make 9.

QUILT ASSEMBLY

1. Sew the blocks, sashing blocks, and cornerstone blocks together into rows. Join the rows as shown.

2. Layer the quilt top with batting and backing; baste. Quilt as desired.

3. Referring to "Binding" on page 17, bind the edges of the quilt.

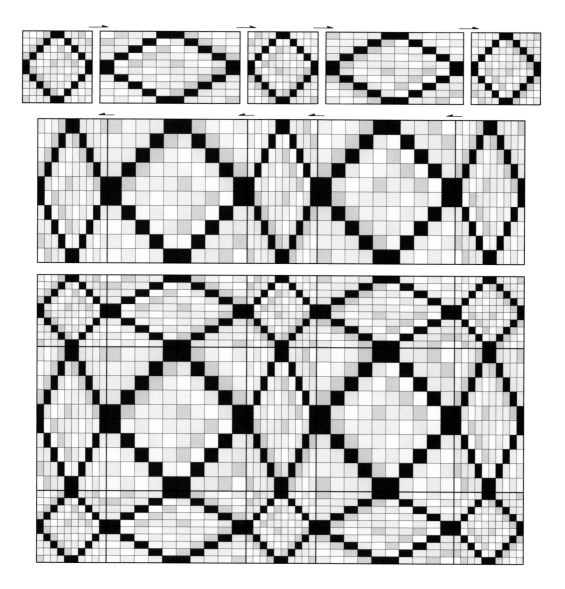

Fall Frolic

By Evelyn Sloppy, 2003

This quilt is tailor-made for fat quarters. Just pick out 11 darks and 11 lights,
and you're on your way. You'll have this quilt stitched together in no time at all.

MATERIALS

Yardage is based on 42"-wide fabric.

- 1 fat quarter *each* of 11 assorted dark prints, *or* 3 yards *total* of scraps, for blocks
- 1 fat quarter *each* of 11 assorted light prints, *or* 3 yards *total* of scraps, for blocks
- 3⅝ yards of fabric for backing
- ⅝ yard of fabric for binding
- 60" x 76" piece of batting

CUTTING

From *each* of the 22 fat quarters, cut:

- 1 strip, 4½" x 20"; crosscut into 3 squares, 4½" x 4½"
- 5 strips, 2½" x 20"; crosscut into:
  - 6 rectangles, 2½" x 6½"
  - 6 rectangles, 2½" x 4½"
  - 6 squares, 2½" x 2½"

From the binding fabric, cut:

- 7 strips, 2½" x 42"

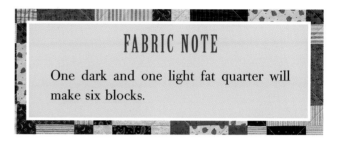

FABRIC NOTE

One dark and one light fat quarter will make six blocks.

BLOCK ASSEMBLY

1. **Block A:** Choose a dark fabric and a light fabric for each block. Sew a 2½" dark square to a 2½" x 4½" light rectangle and to a 2½" x 6½" light rectangle.

CUTTING FROM SCRAPS

If you are using smaller fabric pieces, just cut what is necessary for each block.

For each block A, cut:
1 dark square, 4½" x 4½"
2 dark squares, 2½" x 2½"
2 light rectangles, 2½" x 4½"
2 light rectangles, 2½" x 6½"

For each block B, cut:
1 light square, 4½" x 4½"
2 light squares, 2½" x 2½"
2 dark rectangles, 2½" x 4½"
2 dark rectangles, 2½" x 6½"

2. Using a dark 4½" center square, a 2½" x 4½" light rectangle, a 2½" x 6½" light rectangle, and the units made in step 1, assemble the block as shown. Blocks should measure 8½" x 8½". Make 32 of block A.

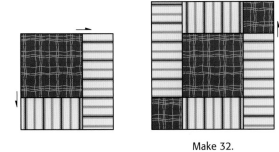

Make 32.

3. **Block B:** Repeat steps 1 and 2, reversing the position of lights and darks. Make 31 of block B.

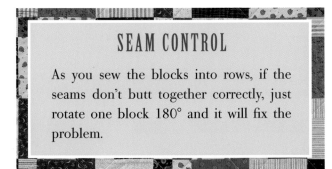

Make 31.

SEAM CONTROL

As you sew the blocks into rows, if the seams don't butt together correctly, just rotate one block 180° and it will fix the problem.

QUILT ASSEMBLY

1. Sew the blocks together into rows, alternating block A and block B. Pay close attention to the direction each block is turned. Join the rows.

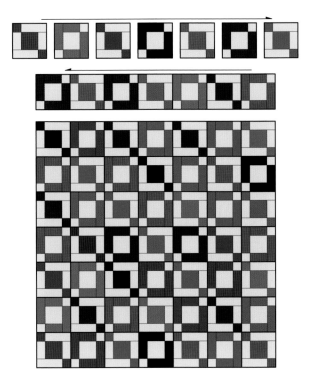

2. Layer the quilt top with batting and backing; baste. Quilt as desired.

3. Referring to "Binding" on page 17, bind the edges of the quilt.

Follow Your Dreams

By Mary V. Green, 2004

Mary loves blues and yellows, so she is right at home with these fabrics.
They have such a romantic look and feel. Simple strip piecing makes quick work of these large blocks.

FINISHED QUILT: 73½" x 88½"
FINISHED BLOCK: 13½" x 13½"

MATERIALS

Yardage is based on 42"-wide fabric.

- 4½ yards of cream print for blocks, sashing, and borders
- 2¼ yards of blue print for blocks, sashing, and borders
- 1⅛ yards of light green print for blocks
- 1 yard of yellow print for blocks
- 5½ yards of fabric for backing
- ¾ yard of fabric for binding
- 78" x 93" piece of batting

CUTTING

From the blue print, cut:
- 27 strips, 2" x 42"; crosscut 2 of the strips into 30 squares, 2" x 2"
- 4 strips, 3½" x 42"

From the yellow print, cut:
- 4 strips, 3½" x 42"
- 8 strips, 2" x 42"

From the light green print, cut:
- 8 strips, 3½" x 42"
- 4 strips, 2" x 42"

From the cream print, cut:
- 14 strips, 2" x 42"
- 12 strips, 6½" x 42"; crosscut 4 of the strips into:
    - 62 pieces, 2" x 6½"
    - 4 squares, 6½" x 6½"
- 6 strips, 3½" x 42"
- 3 strips, 5" x 42"

From the binding fabric, cut:
- 9 strips, 2½" x 42"

BLOCK ASSEMBLY

1. Sew a 2"-wide blue strip, a 2"-wide yellow print strip, and a 3½"-wide light green strip together along their long edges. Crosscut the strip set into 3½"-wide segments. Make eight strip sets and cut a total of 80 segments.

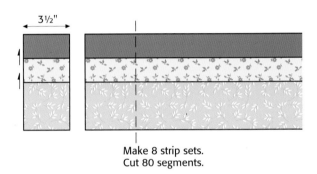

Make 8 strip sets.
Cut 80 segments.

2. Sew a 2"-wide cream print strip, a 2"-wide blue strip, and a 3½"-wide yellow print strip together along their long edges. Crosscut the strip set into 2"-wide segments. Make four strip sets and cut a total of 80 segments.

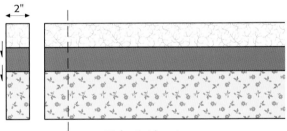

Make 4 strip sets.
Cut 80 segments.

3. Sew a 2"-wide light green strip, a 2"-wide cream print strip, and a 3½"-wide blue strip together along their long edges. Crosscut the strip set into 2"-wide segments. Make four strip sets and cut a total of 80 segments.

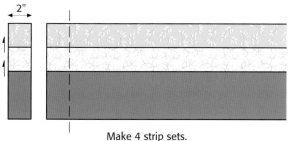

Make 4 strip sets.
Cut 80 segments.

4. Sew one segment from each of steps 1–3 together as shown. The unit should measure 6½" x 6½". Make 80 units.

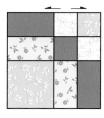

Make 80.

5. Sew a 2"-wide blue strip and two 6½" cream print strips together along their long edges as shown. Crosscut the strip set into 2"-wide segments. Make four strip sets and cut a total of 69 segments. These will be used for both the blocks and sashing.

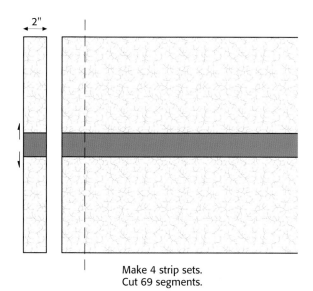

Make 4 strip sets.
Cut 69 segments.

6. Sew four units made in step 4, two cream print 2" x 6½" pieces, and one segment from step 5 together as shown to complete the block. The block should measure 14" x 14". Make 20 blocks.

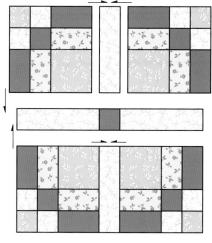

Make 20.

BORDER BLOCK ASSEMBLY

1. Sew a 2"-wide blue strip and a 5"-wide cream print strip together along their long edges. Crosscut the strip set into 2"-wide segments. Make three strip sets and cut 54 segments.

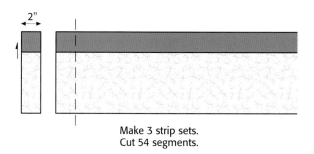

Make 3 strip sets.
Cut 54 segments.

2. Sew a 3½"-wide cream strip, a 2"-wide blue strip, and a 2"-wide cream strip together along their long edges. Crosscut the strip set into 2"-wide segments. Make two strip sets and cut 36 segments.

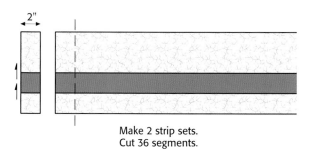

Make 2 strip sets.
Cut 36 segments.

3. Sew a 2"-wide cream strip, a 2"-wide blue strip, and a 3½"-wide cream strip together along their long edges. Crosscut the strip set into 3½"-wide segments. Make four strip sets and cut 36 segments.

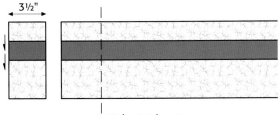

Make 4 strip sets.
Cut 36 segments.

4. Sew together three segments from step 1, two segments from step 2, and two segments from step 3 to complete the border block. The block should measure 6½" x 14". Repeat to make 18 blocks.

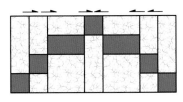

Make 18.

QUILT ASSEMBLY

1. Sew the blocks and sashing units (made in step 5 of "Block Assembly") together into rows. Sew four sashing units and five blue 2" squares together to make each sashing row between the block rows. Sew the rows together as shown.

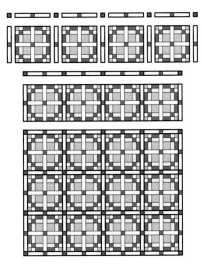

2. Sew together five border blocks and six cream 2" x 6½" pieces for each side border. Sew together four border blocks, five cream 2" x 6½" pieces, and two cream squares, 6½" x 6½", for the top and bottom borders.

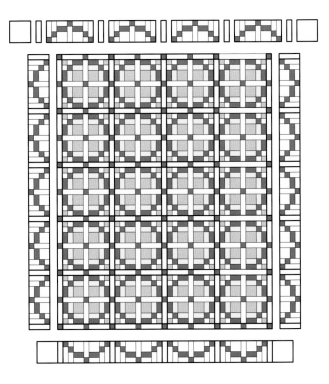

3. Referring to "Straight-Cut Borders" on page 15, attach the borders.

4. Layer the quilt top with batting and backing; baste. Quilt as desired.

5. Referring to "Binding" on page 17, bind the edges of the quilt.

By Evelyn Sloppy, 2003

The striking colors of these softly blended fabrics make this a marvelous table topper or wall hanging.
The quick-to-sew Pinwheel blocks are surrounded by a border of easy-to-make Friendship Star blocks.

QUILT ASSEMBLY

1. Sew the Pinwheel blocks together into rows as shown. Join the rows.

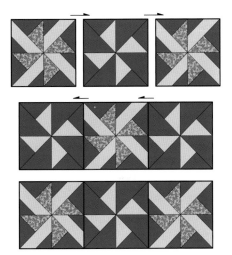

2. Referring to "Straight-Cut Borders" on page 15, attach the light purple 3½"-wide inner border.

3. Retrieve the 20 ready-made bias squares that you saved from the Pinwheel blocks. Trim these to 2½" square.

4. Using the dark purple and light green 3" squares, and referring to "Bias Squares" on page 10, make an additional 108 bias squares. Trim the bias squares to 2½".

Make 108.

5. Sew the light green and dark purple 2½" squares and the bias squares made in step 4 together into rows. Join the rows to make the Friendship Star blocks. The blocks should measure 6½" x 6½". Make 32 blocks.

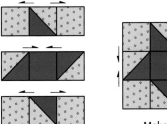

Make 32.

6. Sew seven Friendship Star blocks together and attach them to one side of your quilt. By rotating every other block ¼ turn, all the seams will butt together properly. Repeat for the opposite side. Then sew nine Friendship Star blocks together for the top and bottom borders and attach them.

7. Referring to "Straight-Cut Borders" on page 15, attach the 6½"-wide outer borders.

8. Layer the quilt top with batting and backing; baste. Quilt as desired.

9. To make the quilt as shown with rounded corners, trim the corners with a dinner plate as a guide. Referring to "Binding" on page 17, bind the edges of the quilt. Note that you must use bias binding rather than straight-grain binding if you choose to make rounded corners.

Glory Bee!

By Evelyn Sloppy, 2003

I've never met a red and blue quilt I didn't like, and "Glory Bee!" is no exception. You'll love the fast and easy technique for making perfect quarter-square-triangle units, and you'll also get lots of practice with folded corners.

FINISHED QUILT: 63" x 75"
FINISHED BLOCK: 9" x 9"

MATERIALS

Yardage is based on 42"-wide fabric.

- 3 yards *total* of assorted red prints, *or* ½ yard *each* of 6 red prints, for blocks, border, and sashing
- 3 yards *total* of assorted blue prints, *or* ½ yard *each* of 6 blue prints, for blocks, border, and sashing squares
- 3 yards *total* of assorted light background prints, *or* ½ yard *each* of 6 light background prints, for blocks, border, and sashing squares
- 4 yards of fabric for backing
- ¾ yard of fabric for binding, or leftover scraps for a scrappy binding
- 67" x 79" piece of batting

CUTTING

Before cutting any other fabrics, choose:

- 4 red fabrics for the inner border. From *each*, cut 2 strips, 3½" x 42"
- 4 blue fabrics for the outer border. From *each*, cut 2 strips, 3½" x 42"

Then from the assorted red prints, cut a *total* of:

- 40 squares, 4½" x 4½"
- 31 pieces, 3½" x 9½"
- 4 squares, 3½" x 3½"

From the light background prints, cut a *total* of:

- 40 squares, 4½" x 4½"
- 80 squares, 3½" x 3½"
- 64 squares, 2⅜" x 2⅜"; cut the squares in half once diagonally to make 128 triangles
- 152 pieces, 2" x 3½"
- 2 squares, 4" x 4"

From the assorted blue prints, cut a *total* of:

- 32 squares, 2⅝" x 2⅝"
- 312 squares, 2" x 2"
- 4 squares, 3½" x 3½"
- 2 squares, 4" x 4"

From the binding fabric, cut:

- 8 strips, 2½" x 42"

BLOCK ASSEMBLY

1. Using the 4½" assorted red and light background squares, and referring to "Quarter-Square-Triangle Units" on page 11, make 80 quarter-square-triangle units. Trim the units to 3½" x 3½".

Make 80.

2. Using the 2⅝" assorted blue squares and the light background triangles, make 32 square-in-a-square units. Set aside 12 of these units for the sashing. The units should measure 3½" x 3½".

Make 32.

76 *Glory Bee!*

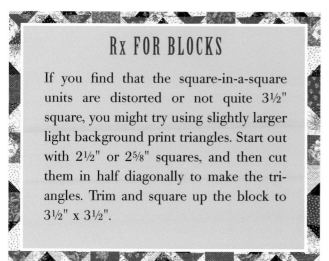

Rx FOR BLOCKS

If you find that the square-in-a-square units are distorted or not quite 3½" square, you might try using slightly larger light background print triangles. Start out with 2½" or 2⅝" squares, and then cut them in half diagonally to make the triangles. Trim and square up the block to 3½" x 3½".

3. Draw a diagonal line on the wrong side of the 2" blue squares. Referring to "Folded Corners" on page 00, sew two blue 2" squares to opposite corners of the 3½" light background squares. Make 80 units. They should measure 3½" x 3½".

Make 80.

4. Sew four assorted quarter-square-triangle units made in step 1, one square-in-a-square unit made in step 2, and four assorted units made in step 3 together into rows as shown to make a block. It should measure 9½" x 9½". Make 20 blocks.

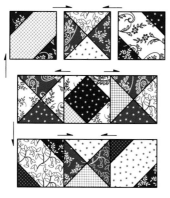

Make 20.

QUILT ASSEMBLY

1. Sew the blocks, the 3½" x 9½" red sashing strips, and the remaining square-in-a-square units from step 2 of "Block Assembly" into rows as shown. Join the rows.

2. Referring to "Straight-Cut Borders" on page 15, attach two red inner borders to the sides. Sew two 3½" red squares to both ends of the top and bottom inner borders and attach them to the quilt.

3. Referring to "Folded Corners" on page 12, sew the remaining 2" assorted blue squares to the 2" x 3½" light background pieces to make the pieces for the middle border. Join in pairs as shown. Make 76 units.

Make 76.

4. Sew 21 of the units from step 3 together for each side middle border.

5. Referring to "Bias Squares" on page 10, make four bias squares using the 4" blue squares and 4" light background squares. Trim the bias squares to 3½" x 3½".

Make 4.

6. Sew 17 of the units made in step 3 together for the top and bottom middle borders. Sew a bias square made in step 5 to each end of these borders as shown. Attach the two side middle borders to the quilt, and then the top and bottom middle borders.

7. Referring to "Straight-Cut Borders" on page 15, attach the 3½"-wide blue border strips to the sides. Sew the 3½" blue corner squares to the top and bottom outer borders and add them to the quilt.

8. Layer the quilt top with batting and backing; baste. Quilt as desired.

9. Referring to "Binding" on page 17, bind the edges of the quilt. To make a scrappy binding as shown on this quilt, cut 2½"-wide strips of varying lengths and sew them together to obtain the necessary lengths.

By Evelyn Sloppy, 2003

I used lots of Christmas greens and reds in this lovely table topper or wall hanging. Making a Christmas quilt really puts me in the holiday spirit. And as an added plus, you'll get lots of practice making bias squares.

FINISHED QUILT: 64" x 64"
FINISHED BLOCK: 9" x 9"

MATERIALS

Yardage is based on 42"-wide fabric.

- 2 yards of red print for side triangles, corner triangles, and outer border
- 2 yards *total, or* 8 fat quarters, of assorted cream prints for blocks
- 1½ yards *total, or* 6 to 8 fat quarters, of assorted red prints for blocks
- 1½ yards *total, or* 6 to 8 fat quarters, of assorted green prints for blocks
- ½ yard of light print for inner border
- 4 yards of fabric for backing
- ⅝ yard of fabric for binding
- 68" x 68" piece of batting

CUTTING

From the assorted red prints, cut a *total* of:
- 26 squares, 5½" x 5½"

From the assorted cream prints, cut a *total* of:
- 26 squares, 5½" x 5½"
- 240 squares, 2½" x 2½"

From the assorted green prints, cut a *total* of:
- 240 squares, 2½" x 2½"

From the red print, cut:
- 3 squares, 6" x 6"; cut the squares in half twice diagonally to make 12 side setting triangles
- 2 squares, 15" x 15"; cut the squares in half twice diagonally to make 8 side setting triangles
- 2 squares, 8" x 8"; cut the squares in half once diagonally to make 4 corner setting triangles
- 7 strips, 5½" x 42"

From the light print, cut:
- 7 strips, 2" x 42"

From the binding fabric, cut:
- 7 strips, 2½" x 42"

PINWHEEL BLOCK ASSEMBLY

1. Referring to "Bias Squares" on page 10, make four bias squares with two red and two cream 5½" squares. Trim the bias squares to 5".

Make 4.

2. Sew the four bias squares together for a block as shown. The blocks should measure 9½" x 9½". Using the other red and cream prints, repeat to make 13 blocks.

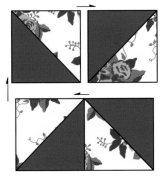

Make 13.

SASHING STRIPS

1. As described in "Pinwheel Block Assembly," use the green and cream 2½" squares to make 120 Pinwheel blocks. Trim the bias squares to 2". The blocks should measure 3½" x 3½".

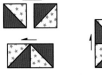

Make 120.

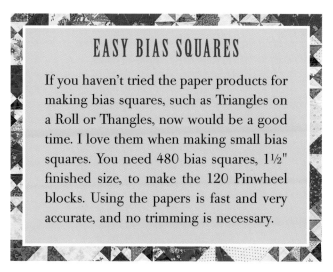

2. Sew three assorted Pinwheel blocks made in step 1 together to make a sashing strip. Make 36 of these sashing strips. You will have 12 single Pinwheel blocks left.

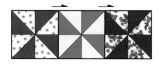

Make 36.

QUILT ASSEMBLY

1. Sew the large red Pinwheel blocks, sashing strips, small green Pinwheel blocks, side triangles, and corner triangles into diagonal rows as shown below. The side triangles will be slightly oversized. Join the rows.

2. Trim the edges of the quilt as described in "Making Diagonally Set Quilts" on page 14.

3. Referring to "Mitered Borders" on page 16, add the 2"-wide inner border and the 5½"-wide outer border.

4. Layer the quilt top with batting and backing; baste. Quilt as desired.

5. Referring to "Binding" on page 17, bind the edges of the quilt.

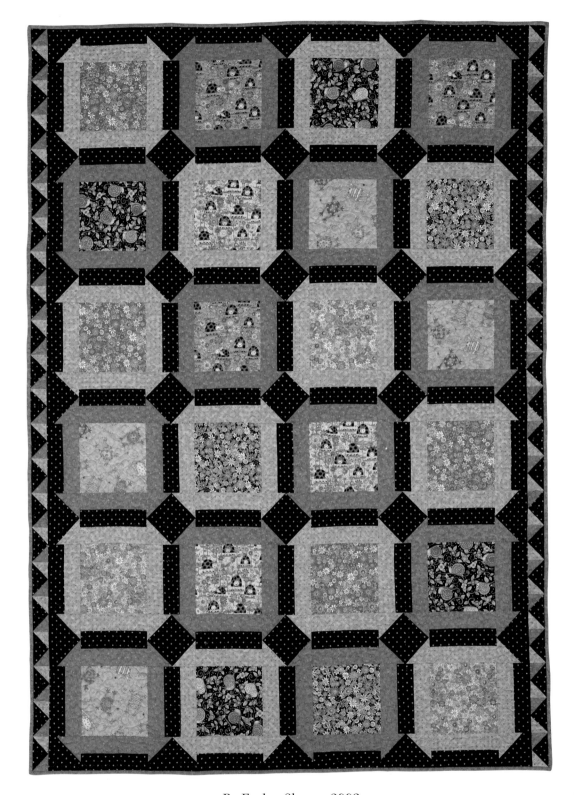

By Evelyn Sloppy, 2003
I never thought I'd go for hot pinks and lime greens, but kids love these fun prints.
The large squares provide an opportunity to showcase favorite novelty prints.

MATERIALS

Yardage is based on 42"-wide fabric.

+ 2½ yards of black print for sashing units and border
+ 1⅝ yards of hot pink print for sashing units
+ 1⅝ yards of lime green print for sashing units
+ ⅜ yard *each* of 6 novelty prints for blocks*
+ 5¼ yards of fabric for backing
+ ¾ yard of fabric for binding
+ 66" x 90" piece of batting

Six fat quarters will also work if they are an ample 18"x 20" after prewashing.

CUTTING

From the hot pink print, cut:

+ 13 strips, 2½" x 42"
+ 5 strips, 3½" x 42"; crosscut into 48 squares, 3½" x 3½"

From the lime green print, cut:

+ 13 strips, 2½" x 42"
+ 5 strips, 3½" x 42"; crosscut into 48 squares, 3½" x 3½"

From the black print, cut

+ 16 strips, 2½" x 42"
+ 5 strips, 6½" x 42"; crosscut into:
  + 15 squares, 6½" x 6½"
  + 16 rectangles, 4½" x 6½"
+ 1 strip, 4½" x 42"; crosscut into 4 squares, 4½" x 4½"

From the 6 novelty prints, cut a *total* of:

+ 24 squares, 8½" x 8½"

From the binding fabric, cut:

+ 8 strips, 2½" x 42"

SASHING AND CORNERSTONE ASSEMBLY

1. **Sashing units.** Sew 2½"-wide hot pink, lime green, and black print strips together along their long edges, with the black print in the center. Make 10 strip sets. Crosscut the strip sets into 38 sashing units, 8½" wide.

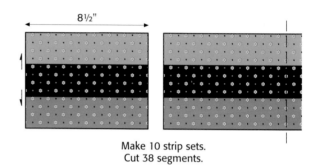

Make 10 strip sets.
Cut 38 segments.

2. **Partial sashing units.** Sew 2½"-wide hot pink and black print strips together along their long edges. Make three strip sets and crosscut the strip sets into 10 segments, 8½" wide. Repeat with the lime green and black print strips, and cut 10 more partial sashing units, 8½" wide.

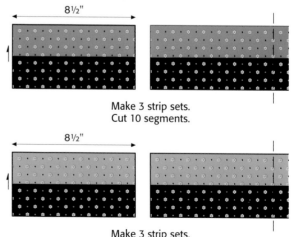

Make 3 strip sets.
Cut 10 segments.

Make 3 strip sets.
Cut 10 segments.

3. **Cornerstone units.** Draw a diagonal line on the wrong side of the 3½" x 3½" lime green and hot pink squares. Draw a second line ½" from the first one so that you can make ready-made bias squares (see page 13).

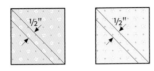

4. Place two hot pink squares on opposite diagonal corners of a 6½" black print square, right sides together, as shown. Stitch on all marked lines. Align the ¼" line of a rotary-cutting ruler along the inner seam line of each corner and trim. Make 15 units.

Keep these sections to be used in the border.

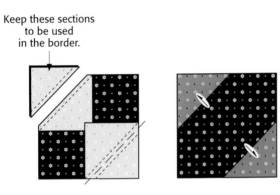

Note: *Keep the sections that are cut from the unit in steps 4 and 5. These are ready-made bias squares that you will use in the border.*

5. Place two lime green squares on the two remaining corners of the units from step 4. Stitch on all marked lines and trim ¼" from the inner seams. Make 15 units.

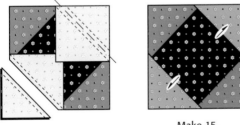

Make 15.

6. **Partial cornerstone units.** Using the remaining hot pink and lime green squares, make units as shown below with the 4½" x 6½" and 4½" x 4½" black print pieces. Sew on the drawn lines, trim ¼" from the inner seams, and save the cut-off units.

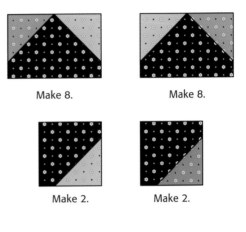

Make 8.   Make 8.

Make 2.   Make 2.

QUILT ASSEMBLY

1. Set the 8½" novelty print squares, the sashing units, and the cornerstone units together in rows as shown. The partial sashing and cornerstone units are used around the outside. Join the rows.

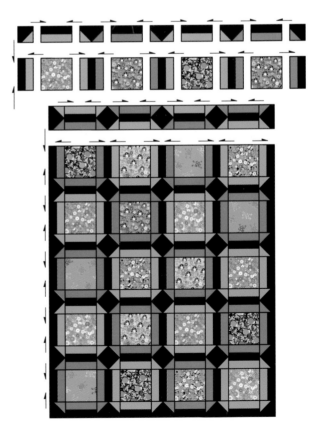

2. Retrieve the ready-made bias squares that were previously cut from the cornerstone units. Trim these units to 2½" square.

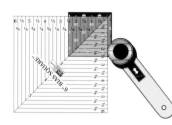

3. Sew 43 ready-made bias squares together for each side border as shown. Attach these two side borders to the quilt.

4. Layer the quilt top with batting and backing; baste. Quilt as desired.

5. Referring to "Binding" on page 17, bind the edges of the quilt.

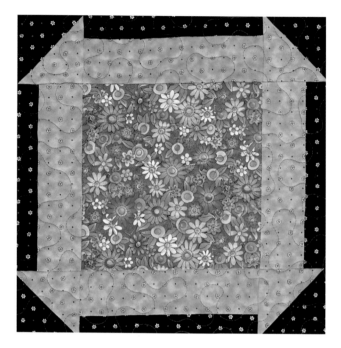

Homeward Bound

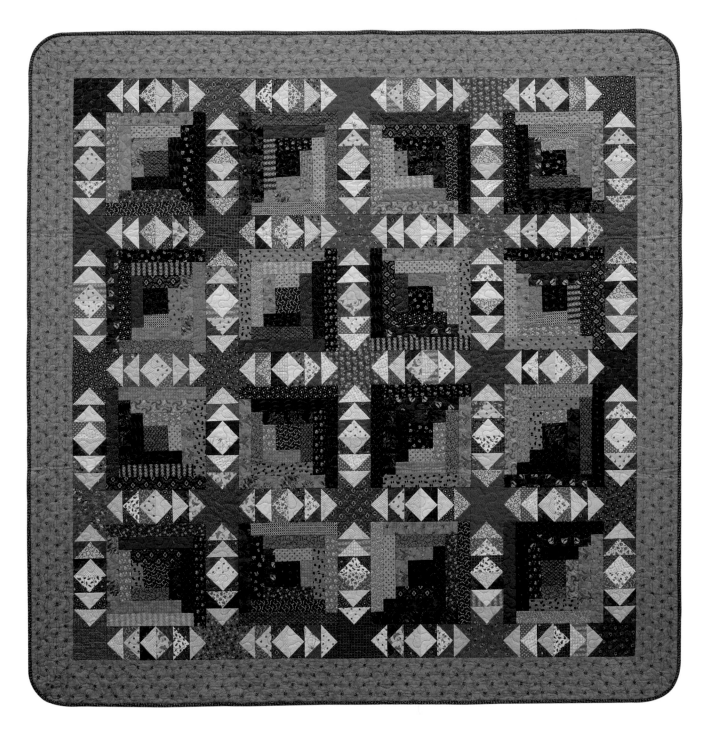

By Evelyn Sloppy, 2004

I can just imagine curling up in my comfy chair with this quilt and a good book.
The charm of the two easy and familiar blocks, Log Cabin and Flying Geese, stitched in wonderful fabrics,
creates a quilt that exudes comfort and warmth.

MATERIALS

Yardage is based on 42"-wide fabric.

- 2½ yards *total, or* 10 fat quarters, of assorted red prints for Flying Geese blocks
- 2 yards *total, or* 8 fat quarters, of assorted blue prints for Log Cabin blocks
- 1¾ yards *total, or* 7 fat quarters, of assorted cream prints for Flying Geese blocks
- 1⅝ yards of gold print for border
- 1½ yards *total, or* 6 fat quarters, of assorted gold prints for Log Cabin blocks
- 5 yards of fabric for backing
- ¾ yard of fabric for binding
- 82" x 82" piece of batting

CUTTING

From the assorted blue prints, cut a *total* of:

- 16 squares, 3½" x 3½"
- Cut the remaining prints into 2"-wide strips (the equivalent of at least 25 strips, 42" long). From the 2"-wide blue strips, cut 16 *each* of the following:
  - 2" x 5" pieces
  - 2" x 6½" pieces
  - 2" x 8" pieces
  - 2" x 9½" pieces
  - 2" x 11" pieces
  - 2" x 12½" pieces

From the assorted gold prints, cut:

- 2"-wide strips (the equivalent of at least 21 strips, 42" long). From the 2" gold strips, cut 16 *each* of the following:
  - 2" x 3½" pieces
  - 2" x 5" pieces
  - 2" x 6½" pieces
  - 2" x 8" pieces
  - 2" x 9½" pieces
  - 2" x 11" pieces

From the assorted cream prints, cut a *total* of:

- 60 squares, 5½" x 5½"

From the assorted red prints, cut a *total* of:

- 25 squares, 4½" x 4½"
- 240 squares, 3" x 3"

From the gold border print, cut:

- 9 strips, 5½" x 42"

From the binding fabric, cut:

- 9 strips, 2½" x 42"

By Evelyn Sloppy, 2003

This quilt is made from 2½" x 8½" strips of fabric. That's it—no fussy shapes to cut. A few simple cuts and the block appears like magic. You'll feel so good about using up scraps that you can go shopping guilt-free to replenish your stash!

MATERIALS

Yardage is based on 42"-wide fabric.

- 4½ yards *total,* or 18 to 20 fat quarters, of assorted medium to dark blue prints for blocks and border
- 3¾ yards *total,* or 15 to 16 fat quarters, of assorted cream and tan prints for blocks and border
- 5 yards of fabric for backing
- ¾ yard of fabric for binding
- 71" x 85" piece of batting

CUTTING

From the assorted blue prints, cut a *total* of:

- 160 pieces, 2½" x 8½"
- 160 pieces, 2¼" x 4"

From the assorted cream and tan prints, cut a *total* of:

- 160 pieces, 2½" x 8½"
- 74 pieces, 2¼" x 4"

From the binding fabric, cut:

- 8 strips, 2½" x 42"

BLOCK ASSEMBLY

1. Sew two blue and two tan or cream 2½" x 8½" strips together along their long edges, alternating the blue and tan or cream strips. Make 80 of these units.

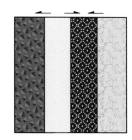

Make 80.

2. On the wrong side of half of the units, draw a diagonal line as shown. Place a marked and an unmarked unit right sides together. Pin the units together, matching seams, and stitch a scant ¼" on either side of the drawn line. Cut along the drawn line. Repeat with all 80 units. Press the seam in either direction. You will have 40 of unit A with light strips on the outer edges and 40 of unit B with dark strips on the outer edges.

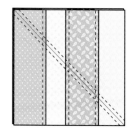

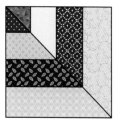

Unit A   Unit B

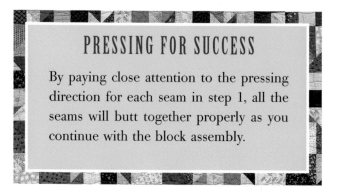

PRESSING FOR SUCCESS

By paying close attention to the pressing direction for each seam in step 1, all the seams will butt together properly as you continue with the block assembly.

3. Cut each unit in half diagonally, perpendicular to the diagonal seam as shown. Make sure the cut is ¼" above the center seam line, even if this means the cut does not go through the two outside corners. It should be close, however. Keep the units together until the next step. The seams in half of the unit segments will have to be re-pressed.

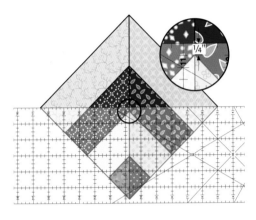

4. Note the direction the center seam is to be pressed in the halves of each segment. Re-press so that the seams in the top half are pressed to the left and the bottom-half seams are pressed to the right. Pair the top half of a unit A with the bottom half of a unit B and sew them together, being careful not to stretch these bias edges. In the same manner, pair the top half of a unit B with the bottom half of a unit A and sew them together. Be sure to mix and match halves so that you end up with scrappy-looking units. Press the seams in opposite directions as shown. Square up the units to 7½" x 7½", if necessary. Repeat with all the segments.

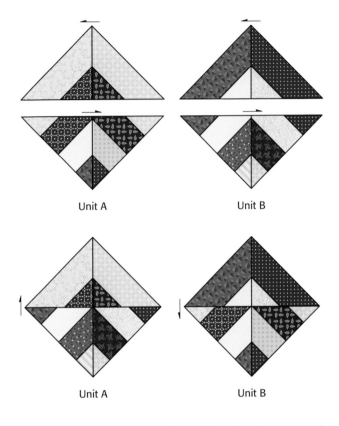

Unit A　　　　　　　Unit B

Unit A　　　　　　　Unit B

5. Sew two A units and two B units from step 4 together as shown. The block should measure 14½" x 14½". Repeat with all units to make 20 blocks.

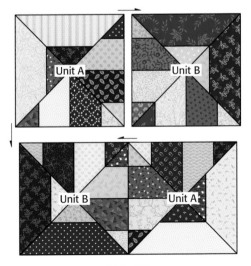

Make 20.

QUILT ASSEMBLY

1. Sew the blocks together into rows as shown, paying close attention to proper placement of the blocks. Join the rows.

2. Sew together 20 assorted tan or cream strips, 2¼" x 4", along their short sides. Referring to "Straight-Cut Borders" on page 15, attach the strip to one side of the quilt. Repeat for the other side. Then sew together 17 tan or cream strips, twice, and attach these to the top and bottom. In the same manner, complete the two blue borders. The number of strips required will increase by 1 with each succeeding border (21 and 18; 22 and 19).

3. Layer the quilt top with batting and backing; baste. Quilt as desired.

4. Referring to "Binding" on page 17, bind the edges of the quilt.

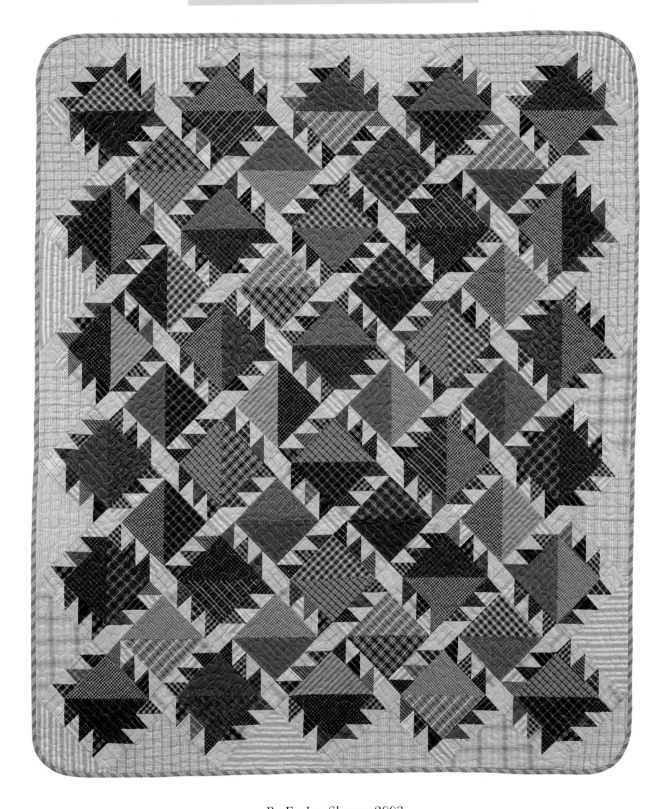

By Evelyn Sloppy, 2003

What guy wouldn't love this cozy plaid quilt on a cold winter evening? All it takes is making plenty of bias squares;
you'll be an expert when you finish this. But remember, they're very easy!

FINISHED QUILT: 59" x 71"
FINISHED BLOCK: 6" x 6"

MATERIALS

Yardage is based on 42"-wide fabric.

✦ 3½ yards *total, or* 14 fat quarters, of assorted medium to dark plaids for blocks and sashing

✦ 3 yards *total, or* 12 fat quarters, of assorted cream plaids for blocks, sashing, and setting triangles

✦ 3¾ yards of fabric for backing

✦ ⅝ yard of fabric for binding

✦ 63" x 75" piece of batting

CUTTING

From the assorted medium to dark plaids, cut a total of:

✦ 50 squares, 7" x 7"

✦ 180 squares, 3" x 3"

From the assorted cream plaids, cut a *total* of*:

✦ 5 squares, 13" x 13"; cut the squares in half twice diagonally to make 20 side setting triangles. You will have 2 left over.

✦ 2 squares, 8½" x 8½"; cut the squares in half once diagonally to make 4 corner setting triangles.

✦ 180 squares, 3" x 3"

✦ 71 squares, 2½" x 2½"

From the binding fabric, cut:

✦ 7 strips, 2½" x 42"

*Cut the 13" squares first and set them aside. Otherwise, you may not have pieces large enough to cut these big squares.

BLOCK AND SASHING ASSEMBLY

1. Referring to "Bias Squares" on page 10, make 50 bias squares with the plaid 7" squares. Trim the bias squares to 6½".

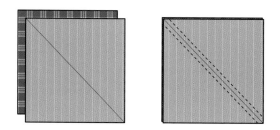

Make 50.

2. In the same manner, make 360 bias squares with the medium to dark and cream plaid 3" squares. Trim the bias squares to 2½".

Make 360.

3. Sew three assorted bias squares made in step 2 together to make the sashing unit as shown. Make 120 units.

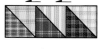

Make 120.

QUILT ASSEMBLY

1. Sew the blocks, sashing units, 2½" cream-colored squares, and side triangles cut from the 13" squares, together into diagonal rows. Pay close attention to the direction of each block. Note that a sashing row and a block row must be sewn together before the side triangle can be attached. Join the rows. Last, attach the four corner triangles cut from the 8½" squares. Trim the edges of the quilt as described in "Making Diagonally Set Quilts" on page 14.

2. Layer the quilt top with batting and backing; baste. Quilt as desired.

3. To make the quilt as shown, with rounded corners, trim the corners with a dinner plate as a guide. Referring to "Binding" on page 17, bind the edges of the quilt. Note that you must use bias binding rather than straight-grain binding if you choose to make rounded corners.

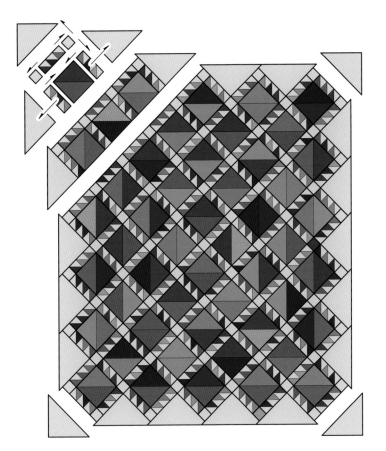

Leftovers Again?

By Evelyn Sloppy, 2004

I love leftovers! But no matter how much I use them, they just seem to keep growing! Does this sound familiar?
If so, here's a quilt with a huge appetite for leftovers. Just grab a good variety of lights and darks,
and your stash is guaranteed to dwindle.

Luck of the Irish

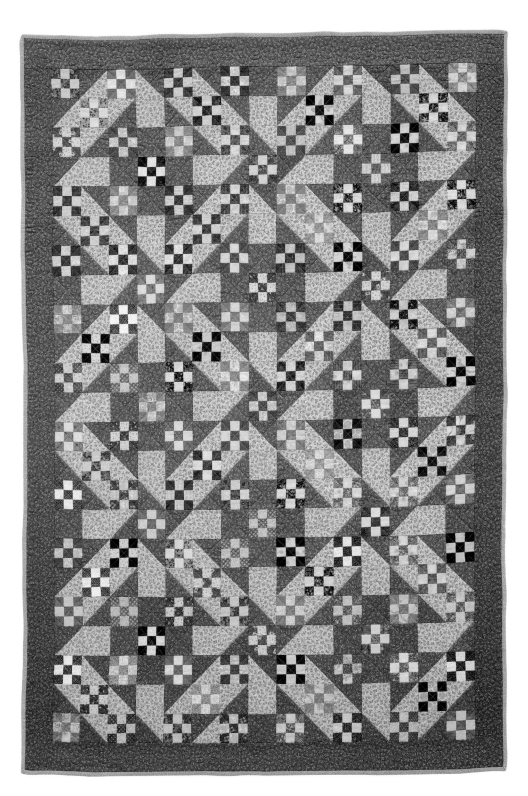

By Evelyn Sloppy, 2003
You don't have to be Irish to gather lots of greens for this scrappy Nine Patch quilt.
I found a happy home for many of my smaller scraps in this lucky quilt.

MATERIALS

Yardage is based on 42"-wide fabric.

+ 2⅛ yards of dark green background print for blocks, sashing, and border
+ 1½ to 2 yards *total,* or 12 to 16 fat eighths, of assorted medium to dark green prints for blocks
+ 1½ to 1¾ yards *total,* or 12 to 14 fat eighths, of assorted light prints for blocks
+ 1⅜ yards of light green background print for blocks and sashing
+ 3⅛ yards of fabric for backing
+ ⅝ yard of fabric for binding
+ 54" x 79" piece of batting

CUTTING

From the assorted medium to dark green prints, cut a *total* of*:

+ 60 strips, 1½" x 21"

From the assorted light prints, cut a *total* of*:

+ 46 strips, 1½" x 21"

From the light green background print, cut:

+ 7 strips, 4" x 42"; crosscut into 67 squares, 4" x 4"
+ 4 strips, 3½" x 42"; crosscut into 38 squares, 3½" x 3½"

From the dark green background print, cut:

+ 7 strips, 4" x 42"; crosscut into 67 squares, 4" x 4"
+ 11 strips, 3½" x 42"; crosscut 4 of the strips into 38 squares, 3½" x 3½". Save the rest of the strips for the border.

From the binding fabric, cut:

+ 7 strips, 2½" x 42"

* If you are using scraps, cut strips 1½" by whatever lengths you have.

BLOCK ASSEMBLY

1. From the 1½"-wide strips of assorted medium green, dark green, and light fabrics, choose a medium or dark fabric and a light fabric for a nine-patch unit. From the dark fabric, cut two pieces, 1½" x 10", and one piece, 1½" x 5". From the light fabric, cut one piece, 1½" x 10", and two pieces, 1½" x 5".

2. Make a strip set with the two 1½" x 10" lengths of dark green and one 1½" x 10" length of light print. Make a second strip set with the 5" lengths, using two lights and one dark as shown. Crosscut the 10" strip set into six segments, 1½" wide, and crosscut the 5" strip set into three segments, 1½" wide.

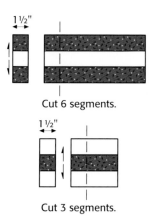

Cut 6 segments.

Cut 3 segments.

3. Assemble the nine-patch units. Each pair of strip sets will make three blocks. Repeat to make a total of 135 nine-patch units. They should measure 3½" x 3½".

Make 135.

MATERIALS

Yardage is based on 42"-wide fabric.

- 2 yards of red print for blocks and outer border
- 1¼ yards of white print for blocks
- ⅜ yard of red-and-white stripe for inner border
- 3¼ yards of fabric for backing
- ⅝ yard of fabric for binding
- 55" x 55" piece of batting

CUTTING

From the red print, cut:

- 5 strips, 3½" x 42"; crosscut into 50 squares, 3½" x 3½"
- 10 strips, 2" x 42"
- 6 strips, 3½" x 42"

From the white print, cut:

- 5 strips, 3½" x 42"; crosscut into 48 squares, 3½" x 3½"
- 10 strips, 2" x 42"

From the red-and-white stripe fabric, cut:

- 5 strips, 2" x 42"

From the binding fabric, cut:

- 6 strips, 2½" x 42"

BLOCK ASSEMBLY

1. Sew the 2"-wide red print and white print strips into a strip set as shown. Crosscut the strip set into 2"-wide segments. Make 10 strip sets and cut a total of 196 segments.

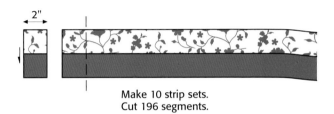

Make 10 strip sets.
Cut 196 segments.

2. Sew two 2"-wide segments together to make a four-patch unit. Make 98 units. They should measure 3½" x 3½".

Make 98.

3. Using the four-patch units and the 3½"-wide white print and red print squares, assemble the blocks as shown. Place the four-patch units with the seams pressed as shown. Make 25 red blocks and 24 white blocks. They should measure 6½" x 6½".

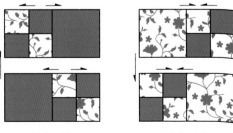

Make 25.   Make 24.

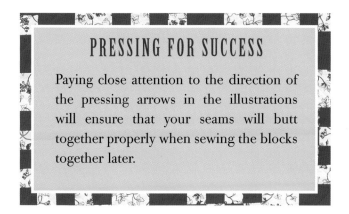

PRESSING FOR SUCCESS

Paying close attention to the direction of the pressing arrows in the illustrations will ensure that your seams will butt together properly when sewing the blocks together later.

QUILT ASSEMBLY

1. Sew the blocks together into rows, alternating the red and white blocks as shown. Join the rows together.

2. Referring to "Straight-Cut Borders" on page 15, add the 2"-wide inner border and 3½"-wide outer border.

3. Layer the quilt top with batting and backing; baste. Quilt as desired.

4. To make the quilt as shown with rounded corners, trim the corners with a dinner plate as a guide. Referring to "Binding" on page 17, bind the edges of the quilt. Note that you must use bias binding rather than straight-grain binding if you choose to make rounded corners.

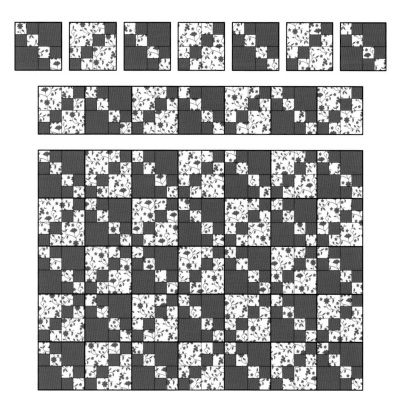

Pine Lodge

By Evelyn Sloppy, 2003

This quilt is such a cozy and warm winter throw. Make it as a gift for someone special on your Christmas list. I've mixed plaids and prints in greens, golds, and blues. Consider using a flannel backing, even if your top is not.

MATERIALS

Yardage is based on 42"-wide fabric.

- 2½ to 2¾ yards *total, or* 10 to 11 fat quarters, of assorted gold prints and plaids for blocks and stars
- 2½ to 2¾ yards *total, or* 10 to 11 fat quarters, of assorted green prints and plaids for blocks and stars
- 2⅛ yards of tan fabric for sashing
- 1 yard *total, or* 4 fat quarters, of assorted blue prints and plaids for stars
- 1 yard of green plaid for border
- 4⅝ yards of fabric for backing
- ¾ yard of fabric for binding
- 78" x 78" piece of batting

CUTTING

Note: *Before cutting any strips for the blocks from the assorted greens and golds, first cut the 4½" and 2½" squares for the stars.*

From the assorted greens, cut:

- 4 squares, 4½" x 4½"
- 32 squares, 2½" x 2½"
- 54 strips, 2½" x 17"*

From the assorted golds, cut:

- 9 squares, 4½" x 4½"
- 72 squares, 2½" x 2½"
- 54 strips, 2½" x 17"*

From the assorted blues, cut:

- 12 squares, 4½" x 4½"
- 96 squares, 2½" x 2½"

From the tan fabric, cut:

- 8 strips, 8½" x 42"; crosscut into 60 pieces, 4½" x 8½"

From the green plaid for the border, cut:

- 8 strips, 3½" x 42"

From the binding fabric, cut:

- 8 strips, 2½" x 42"

*If you are using full-width yardage pieces, cut your strips 2½" x 42". You will only need 24 strips, instead of 54, from the greens and golds.

BLOCK ASSEMBLY

1. Sew three assorted 2½"-wide green strips together along the long edges. Stagger the strips 1½" to 2" apart, to the left. Press the seams in one direction. In the same manner, sew three assorted 2½"-wide gold strips together, staggering them to the right.

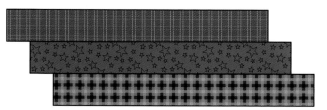

Staggered to the left

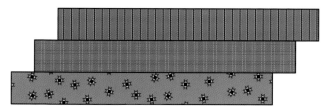

Staggered to the right

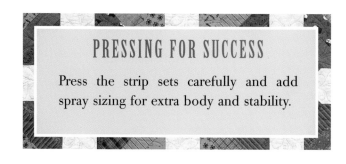

PRESSING FOR SUCCESS

Press the strip sets carefully and add spray sizing for extra body and stability.

2. Place a green strip set and a gold strip set right sides together. Stitch ¼" in from both long edges.

3. Using a square ruler, line up the 8½" mark on both sides of the ruler with the bottom seam line as shown; cut along both sides of the ruler. Rotate the ruler to cut a second block. Continue to the end of your strip set. A 17" strip set will make two blocks. A 42" strip set will make five blocks.

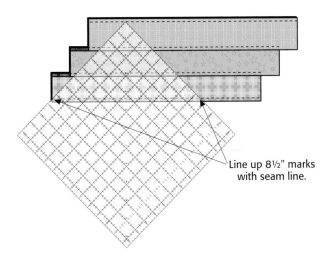

Line up 8½" marks with seam line.

4. Remove any stitches at the point of each block. Open up the block and press the seams in one direction. The block should measure 8½" x 8½". These blocks have bias edges, so handle them with care.

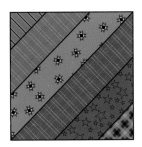

5. Repeat steps 1–4 with the remaining green and gold strips to make 36 blocks.

QUILT ASSEMBLY

1. Lay out the 36 blocks and 60 tan 4½" x 8½" sashing pieces into six rows as shown, paying close attention to the orientation of the blocks. You will make stars in the areas where the sashing pieces come together. Gold stars will go where the green halves of the blocks converge; green stars will go where the gold halves of the blocks converge; and blue stars will go in the remaining areas.

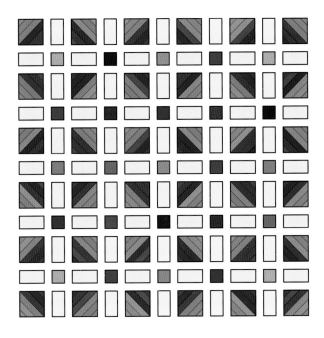

2. Decide on a gold fabric for the first star. You will need one square, 4½" x 4½", and eight squares, 2½" x 2½". Draw a diagonal line on the wrong side of the 2½" squares. Using the four adjoining sashing pieces and the 2½" squares, sew the 2½" squares to the sashing pieces. Refer to "Folded Corners" on page 12.

If you would like to use the discarded corners from the sashing units, see "Ready-Made Bias Squares" on page 13. Draw a second line ½" from the first diagonal line and stitch on both lines. Cut between the stitching lines. This will give you a ready-made bias square. I trimmed mine to 1½" square and made a table runner with them, which you can see in the photo below.

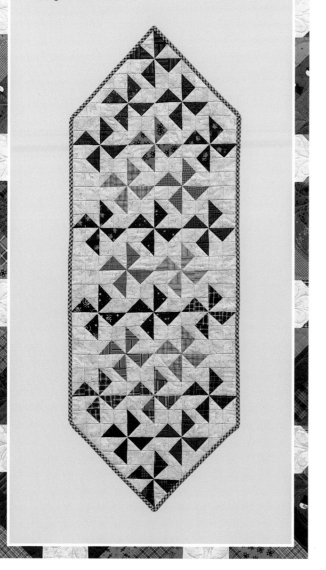

3. Lay the sashing units back in place, with the 4½" square star fabric in the center. Repeat with the remaining green, gold, and blue fabrics to make all 25 stars and star points.

4. Sew the blocks, sashing units, and star centers together into rows. Join the rows.

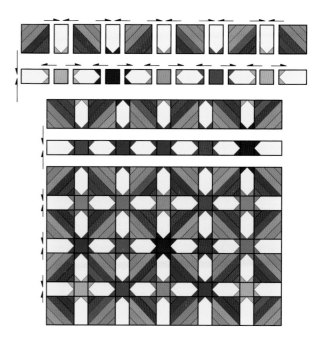

5. Referring to "Straight-Cut Borders" on page 15, attach the 3½"-wide green plaid borders.

6. Layer the quilt top with batting and backing; baste. Quilt as desired.

7. To make the quilt as shown with rounded corners, trim the corners with a dinner plate as a guide. Referring to "Binding" on page 17, bind the edges of the quilt. Note that you must use bias binding rather than straight-grain binding if you choose to make rounded corners.

Polka-Dot Party

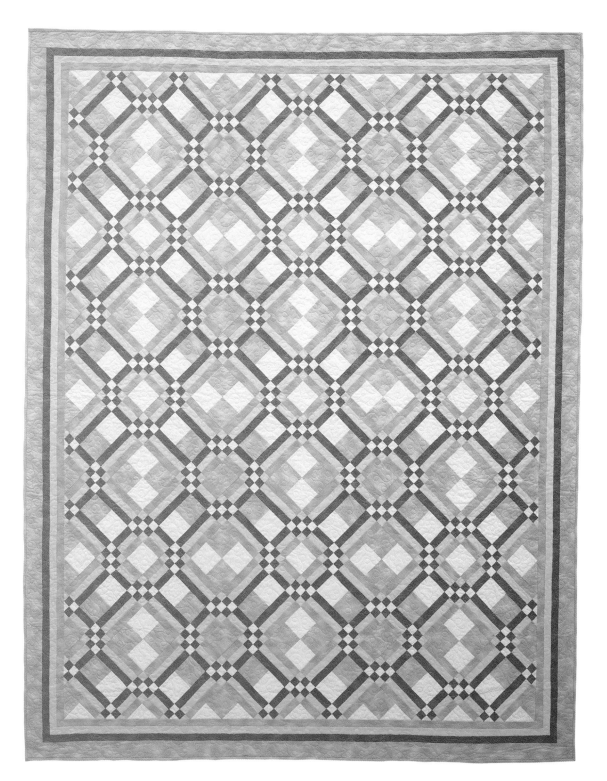

Pieced by Marilyn Fischer, 2003
Perky polka-dot fabrics in this checkerboard quilt make for a winning combination.
The delightful blocks go together quickly with strip-piecing methods.

MATERIALS

Yardage is based on 42"-wide fabric.

- 2½ yards of dark lavender fabric for blocks, setting triangles, sashing, and third border
- 2¼ yards of light lavender fabric for blocks, setting triangles, and outer border
- 2⅛ yards of white fabric for blocks and setting triangles
- 2⅛ yards of yellow fabric for blocks, setting triangles, sashing, and second border
- 1⅝ yards of lime green fabric for blocks, setting triangles, sashing, and first border
- 5⅞ yards of fabric for backing
- ¾ yard of fabric for binding
- 79" x 100" piece of batting

CUTTING

From the light lavender fabric, cut:
- 11 strips, 3½" x 42"; crosscut 2 of these strips into a total of 12 squares, 3½" x 3½"
- 1 strip, 6" x 42"; crosscut into 6 squares, 6" x 6". Cut the squares in half twice diagonally to make 24 triangles.
- 9 strips, 3" x 42"

From the white fabric, cut:
- 11 strips, 3½" x 42"; crosscut 2 strips into a total of 15 squares, 3½" x 3½"
- 14 strips, 1½" x 42"
- 1 strip, 6" x 42"; crosscut into 5 squares, 6" x 6". Cut the squares in half twice diagonally to make 20 triangles. You will have 2 left over.

From the lime green fabric, cut:
- 34 strips, 1½" x 42"

From the yellow fabric, cut:
- 43 strips, 1½" x 42"

From the dark lavender fabric, cut:
- 54 strips, 1½" x 42"

From the binding fabric, cut:
- 9 strips, 2½" x 42"

BLOCK ASSEMBLY

1. Sew the 3½"-wide light lavender and white strips into four strip sets as shown. Crosscut the strip sets into 36 segments, 3½" wide, for the blocks.

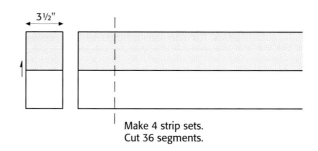

3½"

Make 4 strip sets.
Cut 36 segments.

2. Sew two of the segments from step 1 together to make a four-patch unit. Make 18 four-patch units.

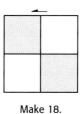

Make 18.

3. Sew 1½"-wide lime green, yellow, and dark lavender strips into 16 strip sets as shown. Crosscut the strip sets into 6½"-wide segments. You will need 96 segments for the blocks and setting triangles.

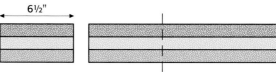

6½"

Make 16 strip sets.
Cut 96 segments.

Posy Parade

Pieced by Lynda Parker, 2003

*Big 15" Pinwheel blocks matched with simple alternate blocks guarantee that this quilt
will go together with maximum speed. Eye-catching teal prints and pleasing pinks,
combined with a touch of yellow, make for a very enchanting quilt.*

MATERIALS

Yardage is based on 42"-wide fabric.

- 3⅛ yards of teal polka-dot fabric for blocks
- 2 yards of pink polka-dot fabric for blocks
- 1⅛ yards of yellow print for blocks
- 1⅛ yards of medium-scale pink print for blocks
- ½ yard of small-scale pink print for blocks
- 4¾ yards of fabric for backing
- ¾ yard of fabric for binding
- 79" x 79" piece of batting

CUTTING

From the teal polka-dot fabric, cut:

- 12 strips, 5" x 42"
- 5 strips, 3½" x 42"
- 6 strips, 2" x 42"; crosscut into 104 squares, 2" x 2"
- 3 strips, 4" x 42"; crosscut into 26 squares, 4" x 4"

From the small-scale pink print, cut:

- 3 strips, 4" x 42"; crosscut into 26 squares, 4" x 4"

From the yellow print, cut:

- 6 strips, 3½" x 42"
- 6 strips, 2" x 42"; crosscut 3 of the strips into 52 squares, 2" x 2"

From the medium-scale pink print, cut:

- 9 strips, 3½" x 42"

From the pink polka-dot fabric, cut:

- 26 strips, 2" x 42"
- 3 strips, 3½" x 42"

From the binding fabric, cut:

- 8 strips, 2½" x 42"

PINWHEEL BLOCK ASSEMBLY

1. Draw a diagonal line on the wrong side of the 26 teal 4" x 4" squares. Referring to "Bias Squares" on page 10, layer the teal squares and the 26 small-scale pink print 4" squares to make 52 bias squares. Trim the bias squares to 3½" x 3½".

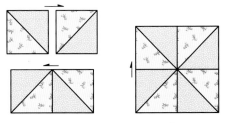

2. Sew four bias squares from step 1 together for the Pinwheel block center. Make 13 pinwheel units.

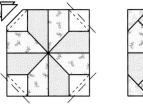

Make 13.

3. Draw a diagonal line on the wrong side of the yellow 2" squares. Referring to "Folded Corners" on page 12, sew these 2" squares to the pinwheel units as shown. The units should measure 6½" x 6½".

Make 13.

4. Sew a medium-scale pink print 3½"-wide strip and a pink polka-dot 2"-wide strip together

along their long edges to make a strip set. Make nine strip sets. Crosscut the strip sets into 52 segments, 6½" wide.

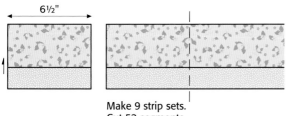

Make 9 strip sets.
Cut 52 segments.

5. Using the 104 teal polka-dot 2" squares, and referring to "Folded Corners," sew the squares to the units made in step 4 as shown.

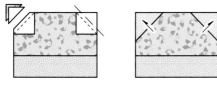

Make 52.

6. Sew a teal 3½"-wide strip and a pink polka-dot 2"-wide strip together along their long edges. Crosscut the strip set into 3½"-wide segments. Make five strip sets and cut 52 segments.

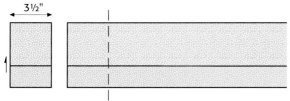

Make 5 strip sets.

7. Sew a pink polka-dot 3½"-wide strip and a yellow 2"-wide strip together along their long edges. Crosscut the strip set into 2"-wide segments. Make three strip sets and cut 52 segments.

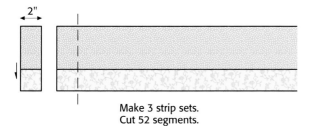

Make 3 strip sets.
Cut 52 segments.

8. Sew a segment made in steps 6 and 7 together as shown. Make 26 units and 26 reverse units. They should measure 5" x 5".

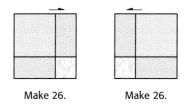

Make 26.   Make 26.

9. Sew units made in steps 3, 5, and 8 together to complete the block as shown. They should measure 15½" x 15½". Make 13 blocks.

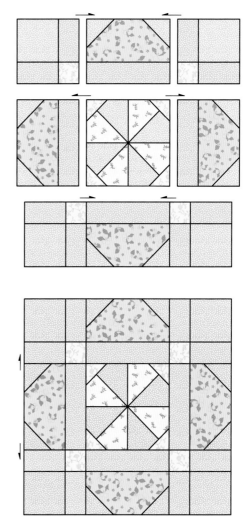

Make 13.

ALTERNATE BLOCK ASSEMBLY

Sew two teal 5"-wide strips, two pink polka-dot 2"-wide strips, and one yellow 3½"-wide strip together along their long edges as shown to make a strip set. Crosscut the strip set into 15½"-wide segments. Make six strip sets and cut 12 segments for the alternate blocks.

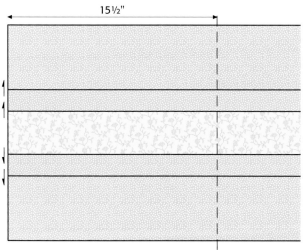

15½"

Make 6 strip sets.
Cut 12 segments.

QUILT ASSEMBLY

1. Lay out the 13 Pinwheel blocks and the 12 alternate blocks in five rows as shown. Sew the blocks together in rows. Join the rows.

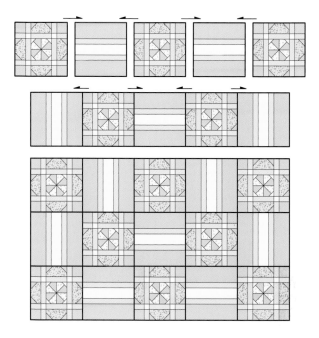

2. Layer the quilt top with batting and backing; baste. Quilt as desired.

3. Referring to "Binding" on page 17, bind the edges of the quilt.

By Marge Springer, 2003
*I like to save even my smallest scraps, and this quilt provides the opportunity for using those
little pieces. Marge chose the country colors of red, blue, green, and brown. They seem
to sparkle when set off next to the red star points and tan background.*

MATERIALS

Yardage is based on 42"-wide fabric.

- 3 yards of tan print for blocks and borders
- 2 yards *total* of red, blue, green, and brown scraps for blocks
- 1⅝ yards of red print for blocks and borders
- 3½ yards of fabric for backing
- ⅝ yard of fabric for binding
- 58" x 73" piece of batting

CUTTING

From the scraps, cut:

- 1½"-wide strips in whatever lengths you have*

From the tan print, cut:

- 17 strips, 1½" x 42"; crosscut 7 of these strips into 68 rectangles, 1½" x 3½"
- 8 strips, 5½" x 42"; crosscut into 82 rectangles, 3½" x 5½". From the remainder, cut 4 squares, 2" x 2".
- 4 strips, 3½" x 42"**
- 3 strips, 3" x 42"**

From the red print, cut:

- 13 strips, 3" x 42"; crosscut into 164 squares, 3" x 3"
- 7 strips, 1½" x 42"

From the binding fabric, cut:

- 7 strips, 2½" x 42"

*You will need the equivalent of at least 35 full-width (42") strips.
**Do not cut the tan middle-border strips until the center of the quilt is put together; the widths may have to be adjusted.*

TWENTY-FIVE PATCH BLOCK ASSEMBLY

1. From the 1½"-wide strips of scraps, choose five strips that are approximately the same length. Sew the five assorted strips together along the long edges. Crosscut the strip set into 1½"-wide segments. Continue making and cutting strip sets until you have cut a total of 90 segments.

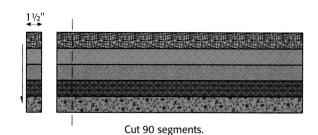

1½"

Cut 90 segments.

2. Sew five assorted segments made in step 1 together to make the Twenty-Five Patch block. Alternate the segments so that the seams are pressed in opposite directions; this allows the seams to butt together properly. Make 18 blocks. They should measure 5½" x 5½".

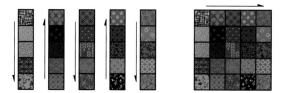

Make 18.

FRAMED NINE PATCH AND NINE PATCH CORNERSTONE BLOCK ASSEMBLY

1. Sew two 1½"-wide scrap strips and a 1½"-wide tan print strip together along the long edges as shown. Crosscut the strip set into 1½"-wide segments. Continue until you have cut 130

segments. In the same manner, sew two 1½"-wide tan print strips and a 1½"-wide scrap strip together. Crosscut the strip set into 1½"-wide segments for a total of 65 segments.

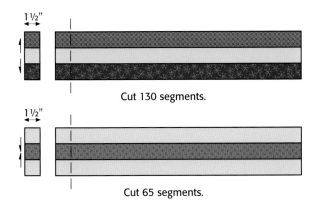

Cut 130 segments.

Cut 65 segments.

2. Sew segments made in step 1 together as shown to make a Nine Patch block. It should measure 3½" x 3½". Make 65 blocks.

Make 65.

3. Cut some of the 1½"-wide scrap strips into 68 squares, 1½" x 1½". Sew two assorted 1½" squares to the ends of a tan 1½" x 3½" rectangle as shown. Repeat to make 34 of these units.

Make 34.

4. Use 17 of the Nine Patch blocks made in step 2 to make the Framed Nine Patch blocks. The remaining 48 Nine Patch blocks will be used as cornerstones when assembling the quilt. Sew a 1½" x 3½" tan rectangle to opposite sides of a Nine Patch block. Then add two segments made in step 3 to the two remaining sides to complete a Framed Nine Patch block. It should measure 5½" x 5½". Make 17 blocks.

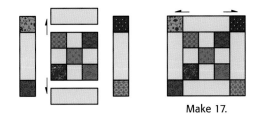

Make 17.

FLYING GEESE BLOCK ASSEMBLY FOR SASHING

Draw a diagonal line on the wrong side of the 3" red print squares. Then draw a second line ½" away from the first one. Referring to "Folded Corners" on page 12, sew a 3" red square on two corners of the 3½" x 5½" tan print rectangles. Sew on both lines and save the ready-made bias squares. See "Ready-Made Bias Squares" on page 13. They will be used in the outer border. Make 82 Flying Geese blocks. Note that these are not true Flying Geese blocks; the corner triangles are smaller than normal.

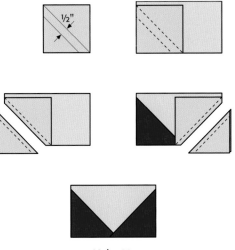

Make 82.

QUILT ASSEMBLY

1. Sew the blocks into rows as shown. Join the rows.

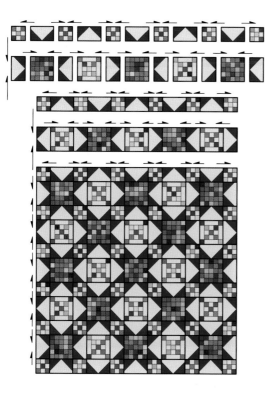

2. Referring to "Straight-Cut Borders" on page 15, attach the 1½"-wide red inner border. Referring to the box below, add the 3½"-wide tan side borders and the 3"-wide top and bottom borders.

3. Press and trim the bias squares cut from the Flying Geese blocks to 2" x 2". Sew 44 of these bias squares together for each side border and

attach them to the quilt top. Sew 34 of the bias squares together for the top and bottom border, and add a 2" tan square to both ends. Attach these borders.

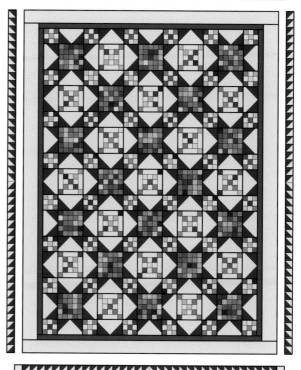

4. Layer the quilt with batting and backing; baste. Quilt as desired.

5. Referring to "Binding" on page 17, bind the edges of the quilt.

The width of the tan border strips may have to be adjusted so that the pieced border will fit properly. After attaching the red border, measure your quilt through the center for width and length. It should measure 45½" x 61½". Adding 3½"-wide tan borders to the sides, and 3"-wide borders to the top and bottom, would bring the quilt to 51½" x 66½", the size you need. If your quilt doesn't measure 45½" x 61½", use the formulas below to calculate the required width of the tan border strips.

Side Borders: Measure the width of your quilt through the center. Subtract the width from 51.5; divide the difference by 2 and add ½". That is the width you will cut the borders. Measure the length of your quilt through the center. Cut the side borders to that length.

Top and Bottom Borders: Measure the length of your quilt through the center. Subtract the length from 66.5; divide the difference by 2 and add ½". That is the width you will cut your borders. At this point, the width of your quilt should equal 51½", so cut your borders 51½" long by the width you just calculated.

Simply Sweet

By Sherrie Boehm, 2004

Sherrie is looking forward to having a few grandchildren, and "Simply Sweet" will be just perfect for one of them.
This quilt goes together so quickly that you might decide to enlarge it for bigger grandchildren!

MATERIALS

Yardage is based on 42"-wide fabric.

- 3 yards of yellow print for blocks, sashing, setting triangles, and border
- 2⅜ yards of blue print for blocks, sashing, setting triangles, and borders
- 1 yard of pink print for blocks and borders
- 4¼ yards of fabric for backing
- ⅝ yard of fabric for binding
- 71" x 71" piece of batting

CUTTING

From the yellow print, cut:

- 4 strips, 4½" x 42"; crosscut into 52 rectangles, 2½" x 4½"
- 13 strips, 2½" x 42"; crosscut 4 of these strips into 52 squares, 2½" x 2½"
- 4 strips, 2" x 42"
- 1 strip, 13" x 42"; crosscut into 2 squares, 13" x 13", and 2 squares, 7" x 7". Cut the 13" squares in half twice diagonally to make 8 side setting triangles and cut the 7" squares in half once diagonally to make 4 corner setting triangles.
- 7 strips, 3½" x 42"; crosscut 1 strip into 4 squares, 3½" x 3½"

From the pink print, cut:

- 2 strips, 4½" x 42"; crosscut into 26 rectangles, 2½" x 4½"
- 1 strip, 2½" x 42"
- 8 strips, 2" x 42"; crosscut 2 strips into 4 rectangles, 2" x 5", and 4 rectangles, 2" x 6½"

From the blue print, cut:

- 2 strips, 4½" x 42"; crosscut into 26 rectangles, 2½" x 4½"
- 27 strips, 2" x 42"; crosscut 1 strip into 4 rectangles, 2" x 3½", and 4 rectangles, 2" x 5"

- 2 strips, 2½" x 42"
- 1 strip, 8½" x 42"; crosscut into 3 squares, 8½" x 8½". Cut the squares in half twice diagonally to make 12 triangles.

From the binding fabric, cut:

- 7 strips, 2½" x 42"

PINWHEEL BLOCK ASSEMBLY

1. Draw a diagonal line on the wrong side of the 2½" yellow squares. Referring to "Folded Corners" on page 12, sew a yellow square onto the 26 pink and 26 blue 2½" x 4½" rectangles.

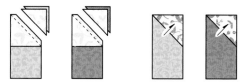

Make 26.   Make 26.

2. Sew each of the pink and blue rectangles from step 1 to a yellow print 2½" x 4½" rectangle.

3. Sew four of the units from step 2 together as shown to complete a block. It should measure 8½" x 8½". Make 13 blocks.

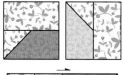
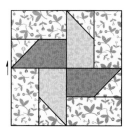

Make 13.

SASHING ASSEMBLY

Sew two blue 2"-wide strips and a yellow 2½"-wide strip together along their long edges as shown. Make nine of these strip sets and crosscut them into 36 segments, 8½" wide.

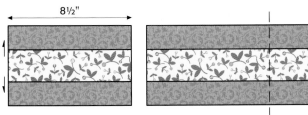

Make 9 strip sets.
Cut 36 segments.

CORNERSTONE BLOCK ASSEMBLY

1. Sew two yellow 2"-wide strips and a blue 2½"-wide strip together along their long edges as shown. Make two strip sets and crosscut them into 24 segments, 2" wide.

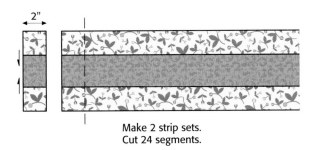

Make 2 strip sets.
Cut 24 segments.

2. Sew two blue 2"-wide strips and a pink 2½"-wide strip together along their long edges as shown. Crosscut the strip set into 12 segments, 2½" wide.

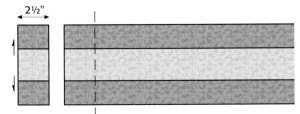

Make 1 strip set.
Cut 12 segments.

3. Sew together two segments made in step 1 and one segment made in step 2 to complete a cornerstone block. It should measure 5½" x 5½". Make 12 blocks.

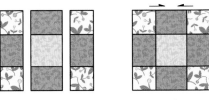

Make 12.

QUILT ASSEMBLY

1. Sew the Pinwheel blocks, sashing, cornerstone blocks, blue triangles cut from the 8½" squares, and yellow triangles cut from the 13" and 7" squares into diagonal rows as shown. Join the rows. Trim the edges of the quilt as described in "Making Diagonally Set Quilts" on page 14.

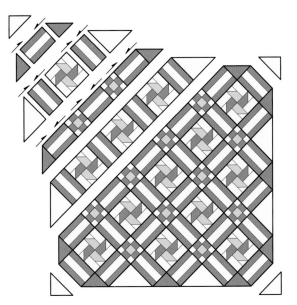

2. Piece the remaining 2"-wide pink strips for the borders. Do the same with the 2"-wide blue strips and 3½"-wide yellow strips. Sew these strips together along their long edges, and cut them into lengths to fit the quilt. Refer to "Straight-Cut Borders" on page 15.

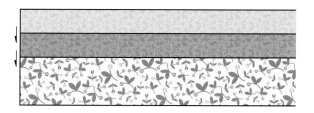

3. Using the four yellow 3½" squares, the four blue 2" x 3½" and 2" x 5" rectangles, and the four pink 2" x 5" and 2" x 6½" rectangles, assemble the four corner border blocks as shown. They should measure 6½" x 6½".

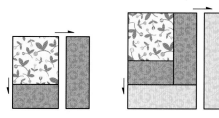

Make 4.

4. Sew the corner blocks to each end of the top and bottom borders. Attach the two side borders first, and then the top and bottom borders.

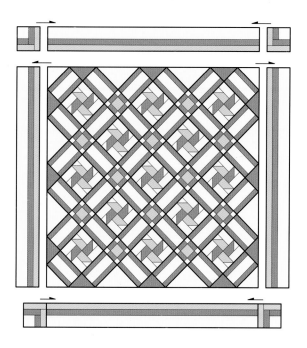

5. Layer the quilt with batting and backing; baste. Quilt as desired.

6. Referring to "Binding" on page 17, bind the edges of the quilt.

By Evelyn Sloppy, 2003

*The soft, warm colors in this homey quilt are just as inviting as flannel. Look closely and you'll see
that all the blocks are the same—only the color placement is different. The intriguing blocks go together quickly,
making this an excellent weekend project.*

MATERIALS

Yardage is based on 42"-wide fabric.

- 1¾ yards of dark green print for blocks
- 1¾ yards of light green print for blocks
- 1¾ yards of pink print for blocks
- 1¾ yards of yellow print for blocks
- 5½ yards of fabric for backing
- ¾ yard of fabric for binding
- 70" x 92" piece of batting

CUTTING

From the dark green print, cut:

- 16 strips, 3½" x 42"

From the light green print, cut:

- 16 strips, 3½" x 42"

From the pink print, cut:

- 16 strips, 3½" x 42"

From the yellow print, cut:

- 16 strips, 3½" x 42"

From the binding fabric, cut:

- 8 strips, 2½" x 42"

BLOCK ASSEMBLY

1. Sew a dark green and a light green 3½"-wide strip together along their long edges. Make 16 strip sets and crosscut them into 96 segments, 6½" wide.

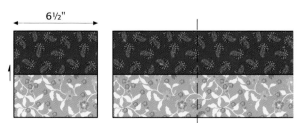

6½"

Make 16 strip sets.
Cut 96 segments.

2. In the same manner, sew a pink and a yellow 3½"-wide strip together. Make 16 strip sets and crosscut them into 96 segments, 6½" wide.

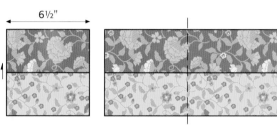

6½"

Make 16 strip sets.
Cut 96 segments.

3. Draw a diagonal line on the wrong side of the pink and yellow units. Place a pink and yellow unit with a green unit, right sides together as shown, with the yellow fabric on top of the dark green fabric. Match the seams at both sides and pin to secure. Stitch a scant ¼" seam on both sides of the drawn line. Cut along the drawn line and press each unit open. Note that you will have 2 different units, A and B. Make 96 each of unit A and unit B.

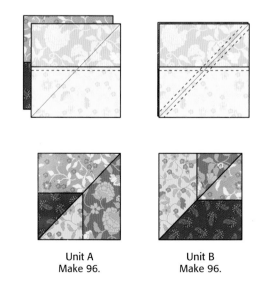

Unit A
Make 96.

Unit B
Make 96.

MATERIALS

Yardage is based on 42"-wide fabric.

- 4½ yards of pale green print for blocks and outer border
- 3½ yards *total,* or 14 fat quarters, of assorted floral prints for blocks
- ⅝ yard of yellow print for inner border
- 5½ yards of fabric for backing
- ¾ yard of fabric for binding
- 79" x 96" piece of batting

CUTTING

From the assorted floral prints, cut a *total* of:

- 40 strips, 3½" x 21"
- 20 strips, 2" x 21"
- 40 pieces, 2" x 8"
- 10 squares, 2" x 2"

From the pale green print, cut:

- 20 strips, 3½" x 42"; cut in half to make 40 strips, 3½" x 21"
- 10 strips, 2" x 42"; cut in half to make 20 strips, 2" x 21"
- 9 strips, 2" x 42"; crosscut into:
  - 40 pieces, 2" x 8"
  - 10 squares, 2" x 2"
  - 9 strips, 3½" x 42"

From the yellow print, cut:

- 8 strips, 2" x 42"

From the binding fabric, cut:

- 9 strips, 2½" x 42"

BLOCK ASSEMBLY

1. Sew together two assorted 3½"-wide floral strips and a pale green 2"-wide strip along their long edges to make a strip set as shown. Make 20 strip sets and crosscut them into a total of 80 segments, 3½" wide, and 40 segments, 2" wide.

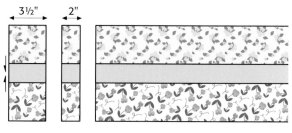

Make 20 strip sets.
Cut 80 segments, 3½" wide, and 40 segments, 2" wide.

2. Sew together a floral 2"-wide strip and two pale green 3½"-wide strips to make a strip set as shown. Make 20 strip sets and crosscut them into a total of 80 segments, 3½" wide, and 40 segments, 2" wide.

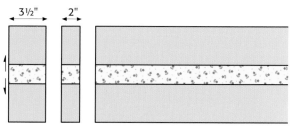

Make 20 strip sets.
Cut 80 segments, 3½" wide, and 40 segments, 2" wide.

3. **Block A:** Sew together two 3½"-wide segments made in step 1 and one 2"-wide segment made in step 2 to make a unit. It should measure 8" x 8". Make 40 units.

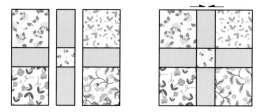

Make 40.

4. Using four assorted units made in step 3, four green 2" x 8" pieces, and one floral 2" square, assemble the block as shown. Make 10 blocks. They should measure 17" x 17".

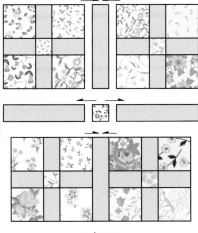

Make 10.

5. **Block B:** Sew together the 3½"-wide segments made in step 2 and the 2"-wide segments made in step 1 as shown. Make 40 units.

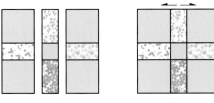

Make 40.

6. Using four assorted units made in step 5, four assorted floral 2" x 8" pieces, and one pale green 2" square, assemble the block as shown. Make 10 blocks.

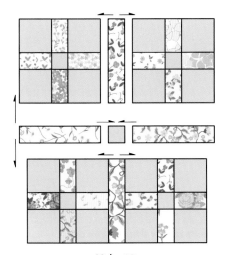

Make 10.

QUILT ASSEMBLY

1. Sew the blocks into rows, alternating block A and block B as shown. Join the rows.

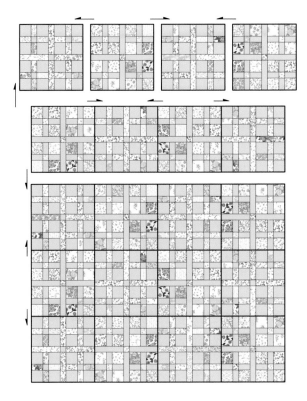

2. Referring to "Straight-Cut Borders" on page 15, add the 2"-wide yellow inner border and the 3½"-wide pale green outer border.

3. Layer the quilt top with batting and backing; baste. Quilt as desired.

4. Referring to "Binding" on page 17, bind the edges of the quilt.

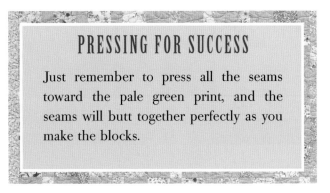

PRESSING FOR SUCCESS

Just remember to press all the seams toward the pale green print, and the seams will butt together perfectly as you make the blocks.

4. Sew together a 3½" background print square and the units made in steps 2 and 3 as shown. Make 60 units. They should measure 5" x 5".

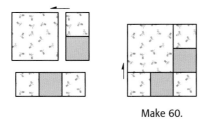

Make 60.

5. Each star will need a 3½" square and eight 2" squares from the same 1930s print. Select the fabric pieces for one block. Draw a diagonal line on the wrong side of the 2" squares. Referring to "Folded Corners" on page 12, sew the 2" squares to four units made in step 1 as shown.

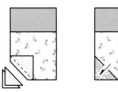

Make 4
for each block.

6. Using the four units made in steps 4 and 5, and the 3½" star fabric square, sew the pieces together into rows as shown to make a block. Sew the rows together. The block should measure 12½" x 12½". With different 1930s prints, repeat steps 5 and 6 to make 15 Star blocks.

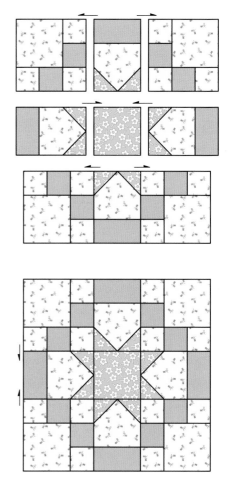

Make 15.

SASHING AND QUILT ASSEMBLY

1. Sew together two background 5¾"-wide strips and a purple 2"-wide strip along their long edges as shown. Make two strip sets and crosscut them into 22 segments, 3½" wide, for sashing units.

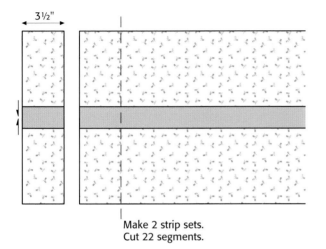

Make 2 strip sets.
Cut 22 segments.

2. Lay out the 15 Star blocks and 22 sashing units into rows as shown. You will make eight more stars in the blank areas where the sashing units come together. Decide on a 1930s print for the first star. You will need a square, 3½" x 3½", and eight squares, 2" x 2".

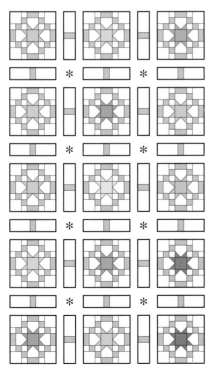

✳ Areas to add stars

3. Draw a diagonal line on the wrong side of the 2" squares. Using the four adjoining sashing units and the 2" squares, and again referring to "Folded Corners" on page 12, sew the 2" squares to the sashing units. Lay the sashing units back in place, with the 3½" square for the star in the center. Repeat for all eight areas.

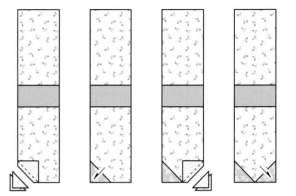

4. Sew the blocks, sashing units, and star centers together into rows. Join the rows.

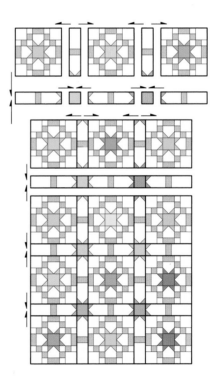

BORDER ASSEMBLY

1. For each border Star block, you will need a square, 3½" x 3½", and eight squares, 2" x 2", from the same 1930s print. From the background fabric you will need four pieces, 2" x 3½"; two pieces, 2" x 2½"; one piece, 3½" x 2½"; and one square 3½" x 3½". Make the star points as you did for the previous Star blocks with the 2" squares and the technique described in "Folded Corners" on page 12. Sew the pieces together into rows, and then join the rows as shown. With different 1930s prints, repeat to make 38 blocks. The blocks should measure 6½" x 8½".

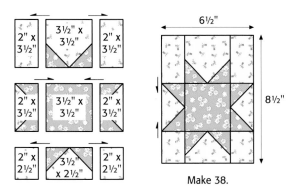

Make 38.

2. For each of the four border corner Star blocks, you will need a square, 3½" x 3½", and eight squares, 2" x 2", of a 1930s print. From the background fabric you will need two pieces, 2" x 3½"; two pieces, 2" x 4"; two pieces, 3½" x 4"; one square, 2" x 2"; and one square, 4" x 4". Make these blocks in the same manner as you did the border Star blocks. Repeat to make four blocks. The blocks should measure 8½" x 8½".

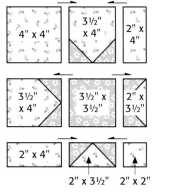
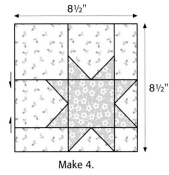

Make 4.

3. Sew 12 border Star blocks made in step 1 together for each side border, paying close attention to the orientation of each block. They are offset so that no points need to be matched. Attach the two side borders.

4. Sew seven border Star blocks and two border corner Star blocks together for the top and bottom borders. Attach these borders.

5. Layer the quilt top with batting and backing; baste. Quilt as desired.

6. To make the quilt as shown with rounded corners, trim the corners with a dinner plate as a guide. Referring to "Binding" on page 17, bind the edges of the quilt. Note that you must use bias binding rather than straight-grain binding if you choose to make rounded corners.

By Marilyn Fischer, 2003

Here's another chance to have fun using those pastel 1930s prints that bring back fond memories for many of us.
This quilt looks complex, but it is made of simple Nine Patch blocks set on point. It's an ideal quilt for a beginner.

MATERIALS

Yardage is based on 42"-wide fabric.

✦ 3⅞ yards of blue solid for blocks and setting triangles

✦ 2½ yards *total, or* 10 fat quarters, of assorted pastel 1930s prints for blocks

✦ 4 yards of fabric for backing

✦ ¾ yard of fabric for binding

✦ 68" x 80" piece of batting

CUTTING

From the assorted 1930s prints, cut a total of:

✦ 80 strips, 2" x 21"

From the blue solid, cut:

✦ 7 strips, 5" x 42"; crosscut into 52 squares, 5" x 5". Cut 2 of the squares in half once diagonally to make 4 corner setting triangles.

✦ 37 strips, 2" x 42"; cut in half to make 74 strips, 2" x 21"

✦ 2 strips, 8" x 42"; crosscut into 10 squares, 8" x 8". Cut the squares in half twice diagonally to make 40 side setting triangles.

From the binding fabric, cut:

✦ 8 strips, 2½" x 42"

BLOCK ASSEMBLY

1. Sew the 2"-wide assorted 1930s print strips and blue solid strips into strip sets as shown. Make 29 of strip set A and 22 of strip set B. Crosscut the strip sets into 2"-wide segments. Cut 289

segments from the A strip sets and 218 segments from the B strip sets.

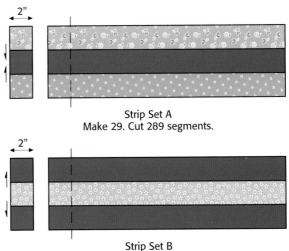

Strip Set A
Make 29. Cut 289 segments.

Strip Set B
Make 22. Cut 218 segments.

2. Sew the 2"-wide segments together to make the two types of Nine Patch blocks. You will need 49 of block A and 120 of block B. The blocks should measure 5" x 5".

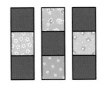

Block A
Make 49.

Block B
Make 120.

QUILT ASSEMBLY

1. Sew blocks A and B, the 5" blue squares, and the blue side setting triangles cut from the 8" squares together in diagonal rows as shown. Join the rows. Add the four corner setting triangles cut from the blue 5" squares. Trim the edges of the quilt as described in "Making Diagonally Set Quilts" on page 14.

2. Layer the quilt top with batting and backing; baste. Quilt as desired.

3. Referring to "Binding" on page 17 bind the edges of the quilt.

Sweet and Sassy

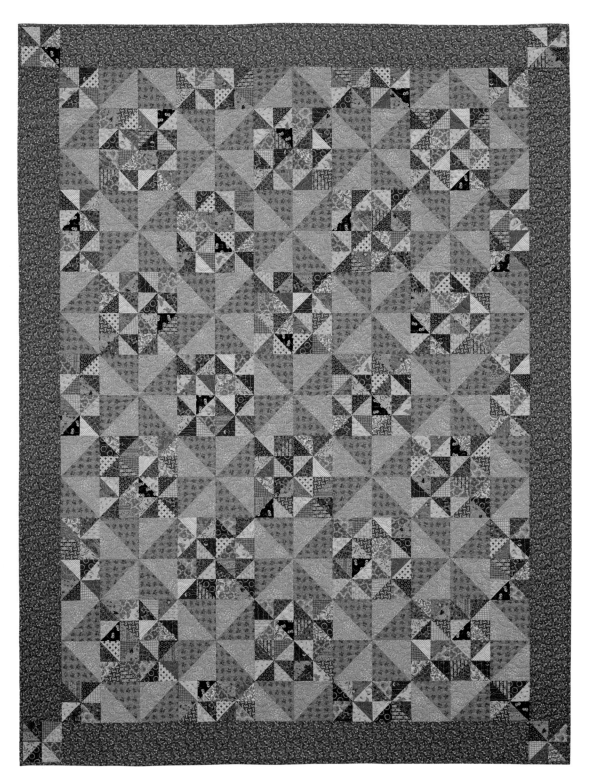

By Kathy Averett, 2004

Kathy loves pinks and browns, and she really has a flair for selecting just the right fabrics for her quilts. Pinwheels twirl all over this quilt, making it look much more complicated than it is. Simple bias squares are all you need to make it.

MATERIALS

Yardage is based on 42"-wide fabric.

- 1½ yards *total* of assorted dark pink and dark brown prints for small pinwheels
- 1½ yards *total* of assorted light pink and light brown prints for small pinwheels
- 1 yard of pink print for large pinwheels
- 1 yard of light brown print for large pinwheels
- 1 yard of brown print for border
- 3⅝ yards of fabric for backing
- ⅝ yard of fabric for binding
- 60" x 76" piece of batting

CUTTING

From the pink print, cut:
- 6 strips, 5" x 42"; crosscut into 48 squares, 5" x 5"

From the light brown print, cut:
- 6 strips, 5" x 42"; crosscut into 48 squares, 5" x 5"

From the assorted dark pink and dark brown prints, cut a *total* of:
- 200 squares, 3" x 3"

From the assorted light pink and light brown prints, cut a *total* of:
- 200 squares, 3" x 3"

From the brown print for the border, cut:
- 6 strips, 4½" x 42"

From the binding fabric, cut:
- 7 strips, 2½" x 42"

BLOCK ASSEMBLY

1. Referring to "Bias Squares" on page 10, make 96 bias squares with the pink print and light brown print 5" squares. Trim the bias squares to 4½".

2. Using the assorted pink and brown 3" squares, pair a dark square with a light square to make 400 bias squares. Trim the bias squares to 2½". Sew 4 of these units together to make a pinwheel unit. Repeat to make 100 units. They should measure 4½" x 4½".

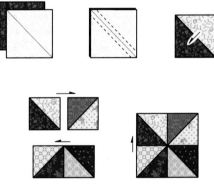

Make 100.

PRESSING FOR SUCCESS

When making Pinwheel blocks, there can be a lot of bulk where the points all come together. To avoid this, I like to press the seams open. Try it both ways to see which you prefer.

MATERIALS

Yardage is based on 42"-wide fabric.

- 3¾ yards of white fabric for blocks and middle border
- 2½ yards *total, or* 10 fat quarters, of assorted medium to dark blue prints for blocks and middle border
- 1¾ yards of blue print for inner and outer borders
- 5¼ yards of fabric for backing
- ¾ yard of fabric for binding
- 70" x 90" piece of batting

CUTTING

From the assorted blue prints, cut a *total* of:

- 346 squares, 3" x 3"

From the white fabric, cut:

- 6 strips, 6½" x 42"; crosscut into 35 squares, 6½" x 6½"
- 27 strips, 3" x 42"; crosscut into 346 squares, 3" x 3"

From the blue print for borders, cut:

- 7 strips, 2½" x 42"
- 8 strips, 4½" x 42"

From the binding fabric, cut:

- 8 strips, 2½" x 42"

BLOCK ASSEMBLY

1. Referring to "Bias Squares" on page 10, make 692 bias squares with the assorted blue and white 3" squares. Trim the bias squares to 2½".

PREFERENCE FOR PAPER

If you've never used the triangle paper products available, this would be a great time to give them a try. Layer the fabric pieces right sides together, pin the triangle paper on top, and stitch on all the dotted lines. Cut apart on the solid lines. The paper is then easily removed, leaving a perfectly sized bias square. When I need lots of these, this is my favorite way of making them. See "Helpful Tips" on page 10.

2. Sew the assorted bias squares together in units of three and five as shown. You will need 70 of the three-square units and 70 of the five-square units. Save the rest of the bias squares for the middle border.

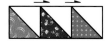

Make 70.

Make 70.

3. Sew two of the three-square units made in step 2 to opposite sides of a 6½" white square.

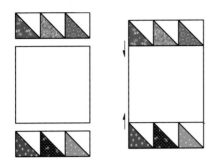

4. Sew two of the five-square units made in step 2 to the remaining sides. Repeat to make 35 blocks. The blocks should measure 10½" x 10½".

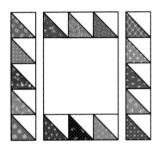

Make 35.

QUILT ASSEMBLY

1. Sew the blocks into rows as shown, paying close attention to the orientation of each block. Join the rows.

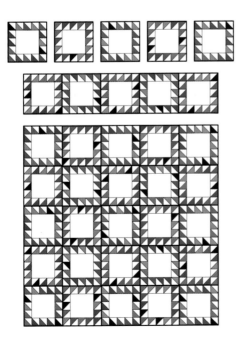

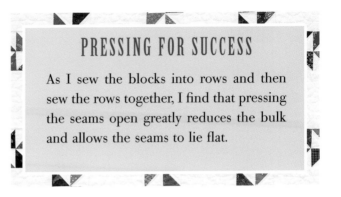

PRESSING FOR SUCCESS

As I sew the blocks into rows and then sew the rows together, I find that pressing the seams open greatly reduces the bulk and allows the seams to lie flat.

2. Referring to "Straight-Cut Borders" on page 15, attach the 2½"wide inner border.

3. Sew the remaining bias squares together for the middle border. Sew 37 together for the side borders, and 29 together for the top and bottom borders. Attach the side borders first and then the top and bottom borders.

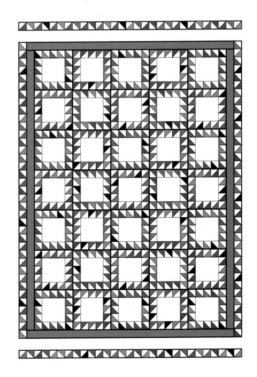

4. Attach the 4½"-wide outer border.

5. Layer the quilt top with batting and backing; baste. Quilt as desired.

6. Referring to "Binding" on page 17, bind the edges of the quilt.

Tutti-Frutti

By Evelyn Sloppy, 2003

Here's one way to transport yourself to the tropics! Make this fun quilt in brightly colored lime greens, oranges, yellows, and blues to jumpstart the summer when winter doldrums are threatening to get you down.

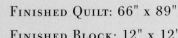
MATERIALS

Yardage is based on 42"-wide fabric.

- 3½ yards of light blue print for blocks, sashing, and border
- 2¼ yards of orange print for blocks, setting triangles, and border
- 1⅞ yards of yellow print for setting triangles and border
- 1 yard of lime green print for blocks and border
- 5⅜ yards of fabric for backing
- ¾ yard of fabric for binding
- 70" x 93" piece of batting

CUTTING

From the light blue print, cut:

- 4 strips, 4½" x 42"; crosscut into 32 squares, 4½" x 4½"
- 2 strips, 5½" x 42"; crosscut into 8 squares, 5½" x 5½"
- 3 strips, 12½" x 42"; crosscut into 24 pieces, 4½" x 12½"
- 9 strips, 5" x 42"

From the orange print, cut:

- 2 strips, 4½" x 42"; crosscut into 15 squares, 4½" x 4½"
- 4 strips, 2½" x 42"; crosscut into 64 squares, 2½" x 2½"
- 3 strips, 3" x 42"; crosscut into 32 squares, 3" x 3"
- 1 strip, 7½" x 42"; crosscut into 3 squares, 7½" x 7½". Cut the squares in half twice diagonally to make 12 triangles. You will have 2 left over.
- 15 strips, 2" x 42"

From the lime green print, cut:

- 4 strips, 2½" x 42"; crosscut into 32 pieces, 2½" x 4½"
- 9 strips, 2" x 42"

From the yellow print, cut:

- 1 strip, 16" x 42"; crosscut into 2 squares, 16" x 16". Cut the squares in half twice diagonally to make 8 side setting triangles. You will have 2 left over.
- 1 strip, 9" x 42"; crosscut into 2 squares, 9" x 9". Cut the squares in half once diagonally to make 4 corner setting triangles.
- 9 strips, 3½" x 42"

From the binding fabric, cut:

- 8 strips, 2½" x 42"

BLOCK ASSEMBLY

1. Using the 5½" light blue print squares and the 3" orange print squares, and referring to "Flying Geese Blocks" on page 12, make 32 Flying Geese blocks. Trim the blocks to 2½" x 4½".

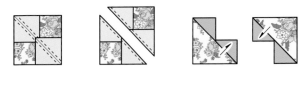

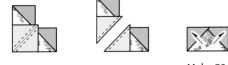

Make 32.

2. Sew each Flying Geese block to a lime green 2½" x 4½" piece.

Make 32.

3. Referring to "Folded Corners" on page 12, use the 64 orange 2½" squares and the 32 light blue print 4½" squares to make folded corner units. Make 32 of these units.

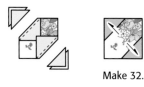

Make 32.

4. Each block requires four Flying Geese/rectangle units, four folded corner units, and one orange 4½" square. Assemble the pieces as shown to make a block. Repeat to make eight blocks. Blocks should measure 12½" x 12½".

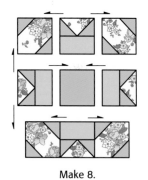

Make 8.

5. Use the six yellow print triangles cut from the 16" squares and the 2"-wide orange strips to make the side setting triangles. Sew an orange strip to both shorter sides of the triangles and trim as shown. Make six.

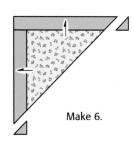

Make 6.

6. Use the four yellow print triangles cut from the 9" squares and the 2"-wide orange strips to make the corner setting triangles. Sew an orange strip to the longer side of the triangle and trim as shown. Make four.

Make 4.

QUILT ASSEMBLY

1. Sew the blocks together in diagonal rows with the 4½" x 12½" blue print sashing strips and 4½"-square orange cornerstones, the corner and side setting triangles, and the orange triangles cut from the 7½" squares. Refer to the illustration. The outer triangle units will be slightly oversized.

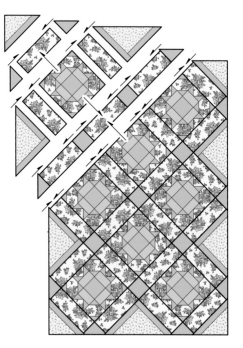

2. Join the rows. Trim the edges of the quilt as described in "Making Diagonally Set Quilts" on page 14.

3. Referring to "Mitered Borders" on page 16, add the 3½"-wide yellow print inner border, 2"-wide lime green and 2"-wide orange middle borders, and the 5"-wide light blue print outer border. It's easier to sew the border strips together and treat them as one border when mitering the corners.

4. Layer the quilt top with batting and backing; baste. Quilt as desired.

5. Referring to "Binding" on page 17, bind the edges of the quilt.

Vintage Patches

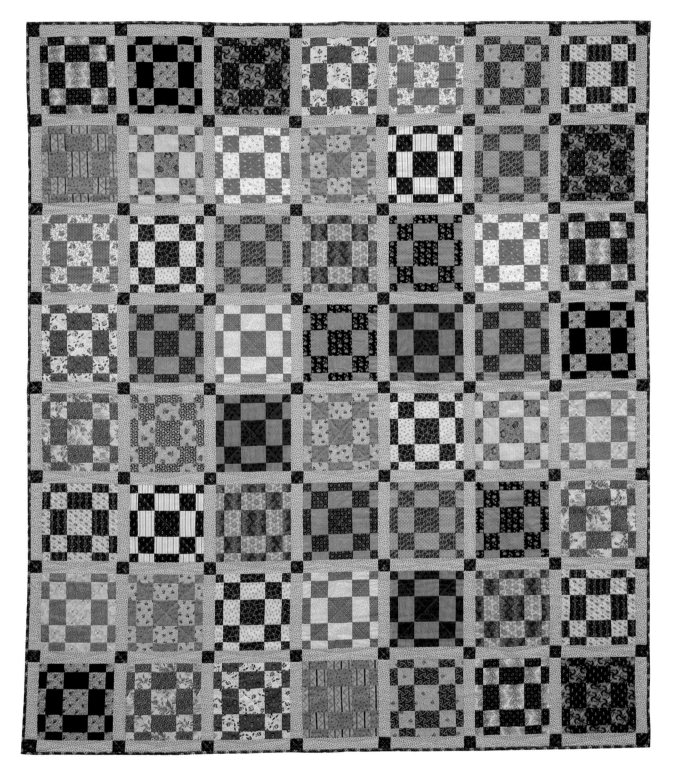

By Karen Costello Soltys, 2004

Karen loves antiques and is very adept at making quilts that look just like those that Grandma would have made.
Civil War prints would be right at home here, or simply draw from your fabric stash to create a classic scrappy quilt.

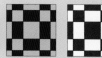
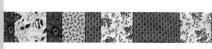
MATERIALS

Yardage is based on 42"-wide fabric.

- 1 fat quarter *each* of 19 assorted light fabrics, *or* a *total* of 4 to 5 yards of light fabrics, for blocks
- 1 fat quarter *each* of 19 assorted dark fabrics, *or* a *total* of 4 to 5 yards of dark fabrics, for blocks
- 2⅛ yards of light fabric for sashing
- ⅜ yard of dark fabric for cornerstones
- 5¼ yards of fabric for backing
- ¾ yard of fabric for binding
- 79" x 90" piece of batting

CUTTING

From *each* of the 19 light fabrics, cut:

- 2 strips, 1½" x 21"
- 2 strips, 2½" x 21"
- 1 strip, 3½" x 21"

From *each* of the 19 dark fabrics, cut:

- 2 strips, 1½" x 21"
- 2 strips, 2½" x 21"
- 1 strip, 3½" x 21"

From the sashing fabric, cut:

- 7 strips, 9½" x 42"; crosscut into 127 pieces, 2" x 9½"

From the cornerstone fabric, cut:

- 4 strips, 2" x 42"; crosscut into 72 squares, 2" x 2"

From the binding fabric, cut:

- 9 strips, 2½" x 42"

BLOCK ASSEMBLY

1. **Block A:** Select a light and a dark fabric. You will need two 1½" x 21" strips, two 2½" x 21" strips, and one 3½" x 21" strip of each fabric. Sew into two strip sets, A and B, as shown. Crosscut strip set A into two segments, 1½" wide, and one segment, 3½" wide. Crosscut strip set B into two segments, 2½" wide.

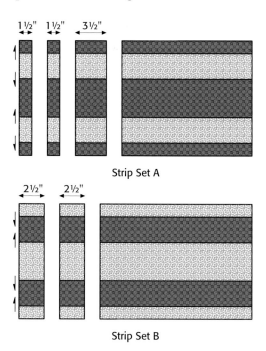

Strip Set A

Strip Set B

2. Sew the five segments together as shown to complete the block. The block should measure 9½" x 9½".

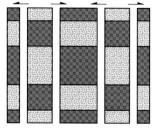

Make 30.

3. Cut the same segments from the strip sets to make two more blocks. Each pair of strip sets will make three blocks.

4. Repeat steps 1–3 to make 30 blocks with the other fabrics.

5. **Block B:** Make block B in the same manner as block A, but reverse the position of lights and darks. Make 26 blocks.

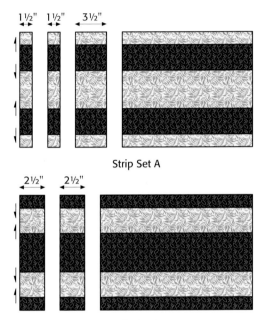

1½" 1½" 3½"

Strip Set A

2½" 2½"

Strip Set B

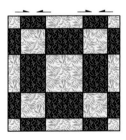

Make 26.

QUILT ASSEMBLY

1. Lay out the blocks as shown in the quilt diagram, placing the block Bs around the outside of the quilt. Sew the blocks into rows, with a 2" x 9½" sashing strip on both ends and between each block.

2. For the sashing rows, sew together seven sashing strips and eight cornerstones, 2" x 2". Join the rows.

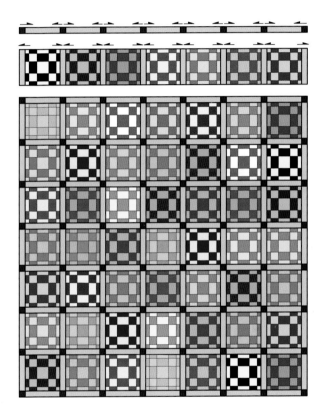

3. Layer the quilt top with batting and backing; baste. Quilt as desired.

4. Referring to "Binding" on page 17, bind the edges of the quilt.

About the Author

Evelyn Sloppy lives with her husband, Dean, on 80 wooded acres in western Washington, where they enjoy country living. They love to travel and hike, and they look forward to visits from their four children and six grandchildren.

Evelyn has been quilting since 1991. Her favorites are scrappy, traditional quilts, but she also enjoys trying new ideas and stretching her imagination. She loves using new techniques that make quiltmaking faster, more accurate, and just more fun. Although she appreciates hand quilting, she finishes most of her quilts on her long-arm quilting machine. This is Evelyn's fourth book with Martingale & Company.